NO AIR GUITAR A
everest

LLOWED

NO AIR GUITAR ALLOWED

By Steve Weinberger
with Sarah Torribio

Illustrations by Andrew Wahrmund

Editing and layout by Waleed Rashidi

NO AIR GUITAR ALLOWED.

Published by Steve Weinberger
steve@noairguitarallowed.com
www.noairguitarallowed.com

Printed in the United States of America.

ISBN-978-0-615-20026-2

First edition: February 2008
Second edition: June 2008

Acknowledgements:

I would like to thank my wife Marna, for her love and patience throughout this four-year process. My two-year-old daughter Keira, for being such an inspiration to me and who has already been to eight concerts. My Dad, for raising me the right way. He is now in his mid-seventies and will not understand one reference in this book except when I mentioned Mel Torme. Dad, you know you are my hero. To my Mom, who is no longer with us, I know you would be so proud. My older brother Chuck, for being my right-hand man at all the concerts even though you would always ditch me for the pit. My oldest brother Bob, for not beating me up when I was a kid and sharing the same sense of humor. My older sister Beth, for always supporting me no matter what. I would like to thank all of my forty-something caught in the "Time Warp" friends. By the way, other bands *do* exist besides Led Zeppelin and The Doors.

I would like to give a special thanks to Sarah Torribio and Andrew Wahrmund for contributing so much to this book. I could not have done it without you guys. I would like to thank Waleed Rashidi for all your knowledge, wit, and for editing/designing the book.

I would like to thank all the fans whom I have mocked from all over the country; especially in my hometown of San Diego. I have had the greatest time committing concert fouls with you over the past thirty years and will continue to do so 'til the end of my time.

— Steve Weinberger

TABLE OF CONTENTS

INTRODUCTION

The alarm goes off at 7 a.m. You look at your clock with a smile on your face. It is only thirteen hours until the concert starts. At least that's what the ticket says—8 p.m. Anyone who has been to a concert knows that, more often than not, it doesn't start on time. The opening band goes on and then the headliner...

All the planning and patience is about to pay off. You've experienced the excitement and anticipation of preparing for a concert, and should now direct your energy toward the next leg of the experience: the social scene. If you are reading this book, you're a rock music fan. If you're a rock music fan, you know that along with sternum-vibrating sound and electrifying ambience, certain givens come with the rock-gig terrain.

For example, you will, at some point in your concert-going career, have beer spilled on you by a shirtless and incoherent man. You will discard your hygienic scruples and enter the sinister zone that is the porta-potty. You will be instructed to turn your head and cough during a pre-concert security check.

Make no mistake: The act of sweltering for two days at a music festival, or of driving to another state to catch your favorite band, is a journey full of spiritual profundity and a million pitfalls. "No Air Guitar Allowed" is intended as a guidebook for that journey. If rock music has no rules, it poses a thousand questions. How can you answer nature's call without missing the encore? How can you ditch your parents at a show without, well, ditching your parents at a show? Is it possible to help make it a kinder, gentler mosh pit? What are the rock faux pas that have the potential to make an entire stadium consider you the most obnoxious human being on the face of the planet?

I feel uniquely qualified to field these questions because I am one of you! I have made every concert foul in the book. I have made out at a Bruce Springsteen concert and worn his sleeveless half-shirt while doing so. I have kicked over a 6-foot-10 guy's beer. I have haggled with a scalper in front of a first date. I have sung out loud at a Wilco show. I have yacked in a porta-potty at an Iron Maiden show. I have fake-vomited my way back to the front of the pit. I have "whooed" through a parking lot in a limo at a Madonna concert. Worst of all, I have closed my eyes tight at a show on numerous occasions, unaware of the thousands of eyes around me as I played air guitar.

Which brings us to the title of our book. Playing air guitar at a concert tops every concert foul that you will see listed. What leads a person to play air guitar at a show? Maybe it's the feelings evoked by the live concert experience. Or maybe it's just that this low-budget musician has consumed fourteen 12-ounce drafts, filled with air and running $10 a pop. Either way, it's a dicey business. If you don't really know how to play the axe, you make a flailing spectacle of yourself and illustrate how far you really are from your rockstar dreams. If you do know enough leads and chords to do a passable imitation of the guitarist, you're halfway to becoming one of the most hated entities on the planet: a mime. If you think air guitar-ing is just a myth, or that the impulse to rock the air has gone extinct, think again. You can encounter this timeworn gesture of musical worship at any show where men outnumber women 5 to 1. A couple years back I saw Ted Nugent at the House of Blues. Five middle-aged guys showed up in suits and ties, high-fiving each other. They spent the entire two hours plastered and playing bad air guitar.

Air guitar has gained a sort of kitsch among modern rock fans, which explains the popularity of fake-it-'til-you-rock it games like "Guitar Hero." In the non-virtual world, there is a great forum for air guitar and that is the increasingly popular sanctioned air guitar competitions springing up throughout the world. However, if your competitive spirit is "strong like bull," confine your practicing to the bedroom.

Writing about air guitar, and all of the fun and funny minutae to be encountered at rock shows, has brought back so many embarrassing, emotional, ridiculous, expensive, noteworthy, fond memories. We all have a story or two about this show or that show and I hope reading this book brings back the same feelings writing this has given me.

The music scene has changed a bit since my older brother was cool enough to take me to my first KISS concert in August of '77. Fans are as likely to hold up a cell phone as a lighter, and terms like emo have entered the national consciousness. However, when you get down to it, dad's old Thomas Guide works as well as GPS. It's still not cool to play air guitar at a show, but it is still very cool to see guys with drumsticks and girls with guitars make a crowd go wild. It's particularly cool if you know a few fundamentals...

—Steve Weinberger

GENRES

Classic rock:
Make new friends but keep the old

There's no statute of limitations on rock 'n' roll. Just ask the Rolling Stones, who first began performing as a skiffle group during the Paleolithic period in a venue called The Cave (which, ironically, was an actual cave). When these grandfathers of rock get back on stage, fans dig those saucy tongue 'n' lips T-shirts out of the closet and go wild.

All jokes about aging rock stars aside, most classic rock groups can still galvanize an audience. Just think: In the quarter-century since these musicians hit their peak, they have continued to play music, ever honing their sound. So, though they move a bit slower, Bob Dylan is still Bob Dylan. Plus, rocker chicks-turned-rocker women like Deborah Harry and Chrissie Hynde still bring it every time.

What *does* change with your garden-variety classic rock act are two key elements: the venue and the line-up. At times, the new setting can feel like a freefall. I caught Missing Persons at a sports arena in the '80s, and saw them struggle to fill a closet-sized club 15 years later.

As far as line-up changes go, it is to be expected that over the years you'll lose a keyboard player or drummer to drugs or, worse, family obligations. What is stranger is when the lead singer, the person everyone has come to associate with the band's sound, is replaced. We're all used to Van Halen frontmen playing musical chairs. Everyone seems to have a favorite VH singer, Diamond Dave or the Red Rocker, and no one could possibly confuse the two.

A relatively new tactic, however, is to pull The Darren Stephens Switcheroo. If you know your "Bewitched," you remember that Darren Stephens, portrayed for five years by actor Dick York, was suddenly replaced by another Dick. Dick Sargent looked so much like York that the change was barely noticeable, especially since it was never mentioned. Furtherore, it was still weird to learn that, not only does father not always know best, there is always a replacement father waiting in the wings.

Journey took a page from the "Bewitched" playbook when the band replaced lead singer Steve Perry with Perry doppelganger Steve Augeri, and then with the Perry-esque Scott James Soto. These switcheroos have been executed so smoothly that unless you're a stubborn Journey purist, you can catch them live and hear the torch song "Don't Stop Believing" sound much like it did back in '81.

This Magic Moment

"I caught the Cure a few years back and Robert Smith was wearing the same messy whore-red lipstick and eyeliner he sported in the '80s. Now that he's 25 years heavier, he looked like Liza Minnelli on a good day. The show was unbelievable, though."

Keep it classy

When it comes to enjoying a classic rock gig, there is one topic even more taboo than the rock 'n' roll invasion of the body snatchers: age. At an oldies-but-goodies fest, be sure to comment on how great everyone in the band still looks, even if they appear to be preserved in formaldehyde. We all want to be immortal, and any acknowledgment that our favorite rock star is aging is tantamount to admitting we're getting up in age ourselves.

Age before doobie

There are some people for whom catching Styx at the local fairgrounds represents the first concert they've been to in ages. These fans are to be congratulated for getting back on the rock-show bicycle. However, if you plan on using the classic rock concert as an excuse to get high for the first time in 30 years, beware of the marijuana your teenage neighbor sells you. The stuff's called chronic now and it's way stickier than the homegrown greenery you smoked that time you managed to catch Cheap Trick at the top of their game. If you just want to mellow out, as compared to embarking on a Carlos Castaneda-style vision quest, just say no.

Modern rock

There's an old saw that holds that wearing the T-shirt of the band you're seeing is terminally uncool. The truth is, most people see no problem with showing your love for the band. The only time you'll get flack for this is if you're hanging out with The Desperately Hip Crowd.

> ***This Magic Moment***
> "Classic rock fans tend to not only age 'with' the band but to age 'like' the band. I remember being at a Crosby, Stills and Nash show a couple years ago and every guy in the audience was like a rocker Franciscan monk. They all had a bald spot in the middle of their heads, and then a ponytail made from what precious scraps of hair were left."

The Desperately Hip Crowd

Members of The Desperately Hip Crowd prefer to sport threads from a bygone era. They might not be caught dead at the local fairgrounds catching a Grand Funk Railroad reunion, but that won't stop them from wearing a vintage Grand Funk T-shirt tight and proud. When a hipster wears a classic rock shirt to an alternative gig, it's not the badge of a lifelong music lover.

It's meant to be ironic. Yes, the giants on whose shoulders modern rockers stand are now delightfully kitsch. No one is cooler than the dude rocking a Lynyrd Skynyrd tour shirt!

Don't do the Time Warp

If you're stuck in the '70s or '80s, be aware that there's a lot of great new music out there. It usually takes breaking up with the wife and scoring a young girlfriend for a classic rock dude to acknowledge that the last hit worthy of singing along with might not be Eddie Money's "Take Me Home Tonight."

Don't be scared off by the absurd splintering of music genres that has burgeoned in the last decade—rockabilly, psychobilly, emo, screamo, alt-country, death metal, folk metal, retro rock, adult alternative... No matter what you call it, it's all rock 'n' roll to me. What's more, it's all just a new name for music that's been around since you were a kid. For instance, emo simply means a pop-punkish goth with a more radio-friendly beat and a more expensive haircut.

Most modern rock fans are open to all kinds of good music—whether it be spawned by eyeliner-sporting, Diesel jeans-wearing fashioncore acts or bands of cerebral English blokes popularized in indie films like "Garden State." However, there is another kind of fan you're likely to spot at a show, though they're not likely to stick around for long: The Indie Guru.

The Indie Guru

You are stoked to see Tool. You picked up their latest album a couple weeks ago and had time to break it in. The upshot? It rocks. In fact—to crib from the bureaucrats in "Office Space," who dig on musical menace Michael Bolton—you celebrate Tool's entire catalogue. The atmosphere is tense. Who isn't dying to catch a glimpse of the dark genius that is vocalist Maynard James Keenan?

The Indie Guru, that's who. This music nerd possesses encyclopedic knowledge of the indie rock scene and an attitude to match. They know that the true test of coolness is how obscure your taste is. To prove it, they have paid $30 not to see Tool but to have seen Quaver, an alt-country-goth band with a lead singer hailing from southern Laos open for Tool.

As performers, the members of Quaver are green as a field of Irish clover. The notoriously bad sound provided for opening acts doesn't help. (The crap sound stems from the fact that opening acts don't have much money so their merch booth clerk/van driver/guitar tech/stage manager/accountant/roadie/caterer is also the sound guy). From your fidgety seat, you can't tell if the group is doing an ironic cover of a Britney Spears tune or praising the Code of Hammurabi in ancient Sumerian. All you know is it sounds horrible. Not so to the discerning ears of the Indie Guru, who takes pride in having discovered Quaver through a freemason-like web of secret music connections. While you go on beer and bathroom runs, the gurus are leaning forward in their seats, if not leaping to their feet in a preemptive standing-O.

Guess what? While the first bars of "Schism" are whipping the crowd into a frenzy, the Indie Guru is hotfooting it out of the venue and into their waiting car. These in-the-know folks would violate their principles if they were seen enjoying a well-known act. If you ask me, they would be staying out past their curfew, the true reason for their opening act craze. Because we all know that this music geek lives with his or her parents. How else could they afford to collect rare 2006 Bolivian-tour-only, 9" marble-colored 78 rpm vinyl EPs while still subscribing to "Never Heard of 'Em" magazine?

Hard rock

The hard rock scene has evolved somewhat, with bands like Shadows Fall and Hatebreed blurring the lines between hardcore punk and metal. Still, the music is aggressive and the fans are slightly volatile. Don't wander into a Megadeth show wearing the same outfit you wore to an AFI gig. Because the minute someone catches sight of those tight pants you borrowed from your girlfriend, they're liable to whip out the brass knuckles they snuck through security.

This Magic Moment

"I used to go to all the metal shows in the '80s trying desperately to fit in, but I never had that rocker look. I would tug desperately at my hair in the back to get the length, but it would only grow thicker and not longer. I would go into Supercuts with a picture of Kip Winger and say, 'I want to look like him' but I would come out looking like Kevin Cronin of REO Speedwagon instead."

In many cases, baseball caps or massive 'fros have replaced long hair, but head-to-toe black is still de rigueur at hard rock shows. It's not just because black is cool. It's been scientifically proven that pastels melt under the pressure of the kind of sonic beatdown you can expect at a hard rock gig. Feel that whiff of adrenaline? That's pure fear, and it comes from the barely-controlled angst of the primarily male fans.

Headbanging is par for the course. If you see a dude with long hair working up a sweat and working out his emotions, consider stepping aside. You do not, I repeat, do not want to be the victim of sweaty headbanging. You will be left with the feeling that you will never again be clean—and you might be right. And don't even think of being the culprit.

Christian rock

There exists a sneaky kind of hard rock or metal that, despite all appearances, is actually Christian in nature. There's nothing wrong with bands of this grand tradition, inaugurated by groups like Stryper and Petra and continuing with such acts as P.O.D. and Underoath. It can feel good to be loud and angsty about your faith, but it's good to know where a band stands, because no one wants to be the idiot caught flashing devil horns while surrounded by a crowd of the forgiven.

Before you go to a hard rock show, check out the band's videos. If there is repeated Christ-like imagery, such as band members receiving a symbolic rainstorm "baptism," or if the vocalist's arms are spread as though he is enduring the trials of Jesus himself, your favorite new group might be religious in nature. Also, check the CD booklet: If the first name in the thank-you list is "Our Lord and Savior, J.C." then you've got verification. If this is the case, practice the still tough-as-nails-looking but less controversial point-at-the-stage-to-emphasize-the-transcendent-coolness move. Your mom may have taught you not to point but this is your best, and blessed, option at this point.

ROCK BUDDIES

Ballads 'n' Balls

It's not just the music you're listening to, but who you're with that can affect your concert experience. Guys, you might not want to bring a male friend with you to a show that has the makings of a chick-flick soundtrack.

All in the Family

Cells and Bics

The desire to rock can hit well before maturity. If you're a kid who wants to see a show but who lacks transportation, you just might find yourself saying something you never thought would come out of your mouth: "Mom, will you take me to see My Chemical Romance?" Parents who aren't comfortable with setting their high school freshman loose into the live-gig world of pounding music, Coors Light on the tap and romantic intrigues on the mind are liable to say yes.

> ***This Magic Moment***
>
> "I caught Foreigner some years back with a friend of mine and we were the only two guys there without a date. Lou Graham rolled out three ballads in a row. By the time he got to 'I Want To Know What Love Is,' I started to wonder whether I'd wandered into an Air Supply show."

Parents just don't understand

To bring or not to bring the folks

Teens, give mad respect to your concert-going parent. As Will Smith, aka the Fresh Prince, once rapped, parents just don't understand. Moms and dads at rock concerts equal a seriously cramped game. If your legal guardians are of the fretful ilk, they will all but keep you at their side with a baby leash. If your parents are relatively chill, the potential for embarrassment is still strong; picture dad flailing to the music like a total dork or mom wearing that too-tight Neil Diamond shirt.

Then there are those silly rules: No lighting up a doobie or getting a friendly-looking 21-year-old to buy you a beer; no making out with that hot piece of action you just bonded with over

that song they've been playing a lot on the radio. Still, keep this in mind: You're lucky your accommodating family member was willing to a) haul your non-driving ass to a distant venue to take in music that, to them, may sound like a harbinger of the end of the world and b) most likely pay for your entry into the world of concert coolness. Though it may take a decade or two for you to fully appreciate the fact, you're fortunate that someone cares whether or not you're abducted by a rock-concert-haunting ghoul. Besides, while attending the Warped Tour with your grandma may seem like a nightmarish alternative, missing the Warped Tour would be even worse.

I suggest you lay out some ground rules. Let your chaperone know that there are some bands for which you absolutely have to be in the pit, and that you wouldn't feel comfortable with them braving that sweaty crush. That way, your parental units won't be in for a surprise when you surge ahead once they're settled. Then, employ some basic parent-child etiquette while you enjoy yourself.

Think of your forays into the great, surging beast that is the mosh pit like you used to think of trips to the ocean. Remember? Your parents let you swim and bodysurf to your heart's content as long as they could still see you from the shore. By all means, join the throng jumping to Pennywise's "Bro Hymn." Then, every 20 minutes or so, head back to say how-do to your parents—or look back and flash them an I'm-more-than-okay smile. It's only right to keep your folks at ease. After all, if they're enjoying the show, you have won the hip parent lottery. Even if they hate the music, they love you enough to sacrifice a red-hot Bunco party for your supreme teen enjoyment.

HE THINKS HE'S GOING WITH US...

TWO HOURS TO GO...

> **This Magic Moment**
> "Back in the '80s my brother took me to a concert. There was pot all around, but he refrained because I was there. Looking back, he must have been so tempted but he played the good brother. Things came full circle when I took my 8-year-old nephew to a concert in 2004. He plugged his ears the whole show and kept asking, 'What is that funny smell?'"

Give 'em enough rope

Parents, we know. You go out of your way to be that cool mom or dad, the one who talks to their kid instead of lectures them—that parent who takes them to that show they can't miss. So, what happens? Your teen's ungrateful face betrays the fact that they find you as desperately embarrassing as if you were wearing full clown get-up. What's more, they keep saying, "I'll be back in a couple of minutes" while sneaking off to the pit or the merchandise table. Most likely, they'll try to extract a couple of dead presidents from your wallet before ditching you. Then it's time for two hours in a "Lord of the Flies" scenario, where adults are absent and chaos rules.

Here's the deal: It's the business of teenagers to be embarrassed by their families. Think back to ages 13, 14, 15 and 16. In your mind, you didn't need your parents, except maybe to provide food and shelter, and to pay for tickets to that rock concert you had to see. Just remember that this too shall pass, and hunker down for what hopefully turns out to be an entertaining musical and crowd-watching experience.

Unless you are seeing a Scandinavian death metal band with an equally homicidal fan base, don't worry about your kid's adventures into the stage-hugging area of a general admission show. Injury and mayhem are exceptions, just as they were when you first started rocking live gigs. Besides, what you don't know can't hurt you. Your daughter may be flirting with disaster, and every member of the opposite sex, in the mosh pit. But in your mind, just picture her smiling and tapping her foot. Just don't smile and tap your foot. She'll die of embarrassment.

The Dating Game

If there is one thing that can get you to a concert at which you normally wouldn't be caught dead, it's the desire to placate or impress a member of the opposite sex. In such cases, it's best to try to appear as if you're into the gig. There are some people who don't even try to disguise that they're only there for their date. Among these folks are two concert archetypes: The Supportive Girlfriend and The Divorced Guy.

The Supportive Girlfriend

The Supportive Girlfriend cherishes no love for the guitar-hero, but you'll find her at a Joe Satriani gig, maintaining a respectful silence while her boyfriend zones out to the music. The tech-savvy dudes in the audience are staring worshipfully at Joe's fretwork, hoping to improve their own noodling. The Supportive Girlfriend,

on the other hand, is barely looking at the stage. Instead, she sits there holding her man's hand the whole time or, worse, gives him a back massage. This public display of affection is annoying, particularly since the guy is so entranced by the show that his girlfriend could be French braiding his nose hair and he wouldn't notice.

The Divorced Guy

Every divorced guy was once a married guy. It is always a shame when a union ends, and it is laudable when a dude gets back out in the scene, embodying the can-do spirit of the phrase, "If at first you don't succeed, try, try again."

What can be amazing to those who knew The Divorced Guy in his past life is how far he will go to try again. If you happen to spot your newly-single buddy at a show, you'll see what I mean. Where he used to wear Dockers, now he's sporting Diesel jeans. Where he used to listen only to Blue Oyster Cult, now he is appreciating the deep meaning in the lyrics of Death Cab for Cutie. Where his wife once stood at his side, perhaps catching heavy-

metal pioneers at such venues as the Indio Municipal Golf Course, there is now a young woman who—when he mentioned his former love for the Blue Oyster Cult—told him that she's allergic to seafood, and that cults are scary.

If you didn't know him in his previous incarnation, how do you recognize The Divorced Guy? Look for a guy at a show who, in comparison to his date, looks like the Crypt Keeper, working hard to mesmerize his new lady with his school-of-hard-knocks wisdom, a touch of newfound spontaneity ("Of course I want to go to Modest Mouse on a weeknight. It'll be fun.") and a whole lot of financial stability.

This Magic Moment

"Though I've never been either The Supportive Girlfriend or The Divorced Guy, I have sacrificed my musical taste on the altar of love. I remember sitting through a Richard Marx concert circa 1990 and finding myself unable to take my eyes off his abundant mullet and tourniquet-tight acid-wash jeans."

There's nothing wrong with this staple character—he may even be a lot like you. The main thing to know is that The Divorced Guy confounds the age curve by being about 20 years older than his neighboring fans. He can bring a certain intensity to fandom because he's busy letting out the genie of living large that's been bottled up for years. He's got the bank account to buy the CDs and the motive and desperation to learn the words and sing along.

The Divorced Guy shares one major characteristic with The Supportive Girlfriend: A love of delivering an intimate backrub in public. Hook this dude up with The Supportive Girlfriend and you're one step away from a Bangkok massage parlor.

Single scene

People who go to a show solo tend to really love the artist. After all, they are willing to face the stigma about going out alone on a Saturday night. However, sometimes it isn't love that prompts someone to hit the town alone but a nasty breakup. You've all seen the girl who bought the tickets, broke up and said, "Screw it, I'm going anyways." She is pissed and bitter and the more she drinks, the more aloof she gets.

Here's the rule: The person in possession of the tickets during the meltdown gets them. The argument goes like this. The guy tells his newly-minted ex to "just sell them since you bought them." If the guy has the tickets in his possession when things go south, he won't ask for her share of the ticket cost, particularly if he broke it off. His best bet is to go to the gig with his new girlfriend, where together they become The Make-Out Couple.

If she hasn't sworn off men entirely, a single woman may also find a last-minute date or meet up with another spurned lover. Between good music, beer and commiseration, they also have Make-Out Couple potential.

Whether it's because our friends are broke or we're in the midst of relationship drama, most of us really agonize over the decision to go to a show alone. Not so for The Creepy Old Guy,

who lives for the chance to scan a crowd undisturbed, trolling for quarry.

The Creepy Old Guy

We all get some lines on our faces and some experience under our belts by the time we hit 40. This doesn't mean you have to get stuck in a music vortex, only listening to music from bygone days. If you stay current, chances are you will one day find yourself as "the old guy" at the show.

There's nothing wrong with that. Feel proud of your die-hard fandom and enjoy the live gig vibe. Just whatever you do, don't be The Creepy Old Guy. You know who I'm talking about, the one who ogles the girls at the gig, taking particular care to chat up the high school and junior college crowd. At his most benign, he looks something like Larry Dallas, from "Three's Company," Jack's sleazy used car salesman best friend.

If this description fits you, remember: You may be young at heart and pure of soul but to someone still rocking their teens, you look as old as the hills and as sinister as a fox eying a henhouse.

Your fellow concertgoers have come to the show to hear great music with their friends. So be the cool old guy instead of The Creepy Old Guy, relax and enjoy the show. When you get home, by all means use up some of your Lavalife credits chatting up women who are single, legal and looking.

SHOW STYLES

Gal Pals

Some performers tend to bring out the ladies—your Ani DiFrancos, your Sarah McLachlans, your Paula Coles, your Indigo Girls, your Joan Osbornes... The last Lilith Fair took place in 1999, but there are still plenty of shows that evoke a powerhouse of gyno-centric energy.

There aren't a lot of rules with regards to these gigs, because four out of five feminists agree that rules are constructs of a male-dominated society. Remember, there are guidelines. First, it is understood that the "woman show" is a time to reclaim lost tribal unity. This means that the girl who keeps bumping into you is not That Bitch (see The Girl Fight) but instead a misguided sister. It is also understood that you are not dressing for men but instead for your own comfort.

Ironically, this guideline creates a lovely scene for the male hetero attendee: bare shoulders and sundresses as far as the eye can see. That's a moot point, though. Because however much the ratio seems to favor you, embracing girl rock does not lead to embracing a girl.

Talent knows no gender or sexual orientation, so it would be incorrect to say a hundred percent of women at an Ani DiFranco gig are lesbians. The percentage is probably closer to fifty, but guess what? The other fifty percent have no intention of hooking up with a guy. Women-oriented happenings represent a time to take a little vacation from the male of the species. This doesn't mean that men aren't welcome at that Chantal Kreviazuk concert. What it does mean is you will feel like a kid in a candy store with no money.

Because there is one cardinal Lilith rule: Don't hit on the ladies when they're channeling goddess energy. Keep your yang in your pants and groove along with the yin energy. You never know. It might be a welcome change.

The Sausage Fest

There are some gigs that bring out the guys en masse. These include: classic metal comeback tours and we-ain't-coming-back-because-we-never-left tours; testosterone-drenched bacchanals like Ozzfest; concerts by any group where the lead guitarist can, in a pinch, play Beethoven's 9th on his axe; and Rush.

If you are female and in attendance at one of these shows, it means that a) you really like your significant other or b) you are a rock-or-die chick who deserves mad respect and cuts in the beer line. It also means that, for once in your life, you just might breeze your way into the ladies room. As far as rules, just follow the what-would-Lita-Ford-do? protocol and have fun.

If you are a male at the kind of show that has been crudely dubbed The Sausagefest, it means you are here for the music. Period. Why? Because there are hardly any women. Those that are in attendance are probably in the bathroom celebrating the lack of lines.

What do you need to know about The Sausagefest? First, binge-drinking is all but a requirement. With this in mind, avoid trying to talk sense into a belligerent fellow concertgoer; it will only end in a scuffle, because his left brain has been deadened by plastic cup after plastic cup of beer. Speaking of alcohol, you might want to say The Serenity Prayer at some point because, in this rarified milieu, there are some things you cannot change. You will find yourself behind a jaw-droppingly tall guy. For some reason, tall guys like to stand, arms crossed, like silent sentinels at metal shows. It gives them a sense of purpose.

It is also a truth to be held self-evident that, if you don't keep a sharp lookout, you will step on vomit on the way to your car. Going to the bathroom is also an obstacle course, like that story where the man has to pick a door, uncertain of whether a lady or a tiger lies behind it, cause half the stalls will be filled with nachos, beer and bile.

This Magic Moment

"I saw Rush recently at a filled-to-capacity amphitheater. The ratio was so typical. There were like 19,000 people there, five of whom were girls."

Despite these inconveniences,

hard rock shows are often triumphant in spirit. One sentiment runs like a river through the crowd: Rock 'n' roll will never die—this is true. Because just when you think that long hair is out and whining is in, you discover that music in Sweden, Germany and northern Europe in general is getting angrier and less homogenized. Sure, and why not? After all, they invented the double-dot umlaut punctuation that lends emphasis to so many legendary rock outfits. Enjöy!

Wherever you go, that's where you're at

Gigs can take place at arenas or bars, or your favorite band may have a set during one of the large music festivals that keep the summer months rocking. While all rock shows share some common threads, each of these venues has its own characteristics.

Bars

Gigs that take place at bars can be some of the best musical experiences, because you're so close to the band. Parking is easier, the atmosphere is intimate and the sound swells the walls of the venue; with the proximity to hard liquor and bartenders who mean business about tips, the drunk-to-sober ratio also increases a hundred fold.

Many bars have a few tables and chairs, or even comfy couches, available to those who get to a gig early enough. Most people tend to stay on their feet throughout a bar show, and this is where genetics can become a problem.

Like all true fans, The Tall Dude takes his rock where he can get it, but he seems to have a special affinity for bar gigs and other general admission shows. It is at standing-room only events where he rises to his full glory.

The Tall Dude

Okay, we get it. That guy who is blocking the sun, not to mention the stage, did not ask to be as tall as Bill Walton. All he wants to do is to enjoy the show. Yet the fact remains that, by his very nature,

The Tall Dude is a concertgoer's nightmare. No one paid $75 plus handling fees to read "Shop at the Kum & Go" on the back of someone's T-shirt all night. (Note: The Kum & Go is an actual Midwestern chain of convenience stores.)

If you are The Tall Dude, it's a drag to know that there are people giving you the stink-eye just because of your height. After all, people go to concerts to leave their worries behind and mellow out with like-minded folks. Just remember the consolations of your increased altitude. You can always see the stage, and you serve as a beacon of hope for your buddies when they get lost in the crowd. There are ways to minimize the impact of your pillar-like dimensions. Know this: All those behind you have carefully positioned themselves so they can peer around you and catch a glimpse of the stage. Every time you move, you are harshing someone's logistical buzz. With that in mind, stay put!

Arenas

Shows at arenas are generally big deals. The sell-out tour is living, seething proof that there are 10,000 people who want to see a band as much as you do. There is a class system at arena shows—much more so than at general admission gigs. Those who have both money and foresight control the front-row seats. They are the Enron execs, natural heirs to the kind of wealth and beauty that you only know about through watching re-runs of "Dallas."

The next time you're in your nosebleed seats, take out those old binoculars you borrowed from dad. Exactly one mile ahead you'll spot them, a group of people as exotic as the band you're seeing. They are The Concert Snobs.

The Concert Snobs

You often find yourself driving from the 'burbs to the city center when catching a show. The Concert Snob doesn't have to drive to the city center. They live there, usually in a loft. In fact, The Concert Snob is more than a little convinced that the city centers around them.

The Concert Snob always has fantastic seats, usually in the front five rows. Aware of this prominence, they always look pulled together. Even if they're wearing jeans and a T-shirt, something in the way their clothes hang betrays the fact that their outfit costs more than the paycheck you got an advance for to get your tickets. With seats this great, members of the respective Whoo Crews and your typical Bro-Magnon would feel like they were in heaven and cheer loud as hell. The Concert Snob, however, has cultivated an unimpressed demeanor for so long that he or she is now unable to discard it.

As compared to the average lucky bastard with good seats, who reaches for Thom Yorke's hand or the flute of Ian Anderson of Jethro Tull, The Concert Snob acts like they've been forced to endure an event as uninspiring as a life insurance consultation. This character, who comes in two forms—as part of a snotty pair or a member of a pompous pack—will talk to their friends, chat on the cell phone and spend a lot of time looking as bored as possible. No clapping, no screaming.

There is a time when you can benefit from The Concert Snob's apathy, and that's in the case of pricey season tickets. If a show is, how you say, uninspiring, he or she is liable to stay home and play it cool. When this happens, it is the perfect time to sneak up to the better seats. That's when you can really whoop it up. Because not only are you so close to the stage that you can take a sip from the bassist's beer, you can also bother your new neighbor, who is likely to be a Concert Snob, by putting your arm around his or her shoulder and giving your biggest "Whoooooooo!"

Terrified of looking like a normal mortal, they may just slink out of the concert altogether, in search of the stiff drink they seem to be craving.

Festivals

Festivals offer a whole lot of bang for your buck. There's nothing cooler than having a day or two set aside to catch a steady line-up of some of the best music around. They also provide the chance to take in the rays of the sun while getting your rock on al fresco-style. However, festivals are also logistically complex and should be planned for accordingly. You may need to drive for a couple hours to get to the venue and if you're taking in a two-day show, you'll need accommodations, be it a Woodstock-style tent or a local hotel. You'll need to provide for your bodily needs with sun block and maybe even extra toilet paper. Plus, you'll need a mind-boggling supply of cash on hand because—as hippy-like as the whole music under the sun and stars sounds—nothing can bleed your wallet dry faster than a musical festival.

Attack of the porta-potty

There have been some wonderful developments in porta-potty technology, from in-the-can pumps dispensing hand sanitizer to outdoor portable sinks where water flows with the tap of your feet. However, there is one thing about chemical toilets that hasn't changed since porta-potties served seized-up flower children at the original Woodstock: Instead of pulling a hygienic disappearing act and flowing away, everyone's leavings drop a couple feet down, where it stays until the show's over and the guy with the worst job in the world suctions it clean.

Sometimes you can ignore this fact, particularly if you are one of the early birds to first grace the line of blue plastic portals parked outside of venues for the benefit of tailgaters. If you have to use a porta-potty a couple hours into an event, there is no chemical disinfectant/deodorizer that can hide the smell of waste.

So how do you make your jaunt to the John bearable? First, make like you are on a rope ladder stretched across a gaping canyon. Whatever you do, don't look down because your courage is sure to fail. Of course, that's a tall order if you're a guy taking a leak. Consider aiming quickly, then staring fixedly at the back wall of the toilet. The idea is to minimize the time you have to spend

staring at a multicolored collection of human detritus.

Second, hold your breath. Hold your breath as long as possible. Swimmers have an advantage here and, with that in mind, you might want to consider going into training in the weeks before a concert. Then, if you have to get some air, make it fast and make it through your mouth. In fact, try to make the whole distasteful operation fast.

If you are at outdoor festival, all or most of your "business" will take place in a portable toilet. What with the large volume of gotta-go traffic and festival weather heat, the chemical toilets can take on a nightmarish quality. As bad as it is, you've got to be a trooper because your bladder and bowels don't take a siesta just because the accommodations are gross. Tuck some toilet paper into your bag and maybe even some hand wipes and you'll emerge from your session relatively unscathed.

Some good may even come from the stinky experience, in the form of an improved sense of appreciation for what you have. Because when you get home, the porcelain wonder that is your flush toilet will truly look like a throne in comparison. And guess who's the king or queen? You, that's who!

The Rock Lobster

It doesn't matter if you are redheaded and Irish and, as funnyman Conan O'Brien says, "should be living in a peat bog." When preparing for a festival, it's all too easy to forget the sun block. Your mind may be occupied with trying to sneak in water bottles and various herbs, you may not want to admit just what a scorcher you're in for or—worse yet, you may be saying those famous last words: "Hey, I could use a little color anyway."

Here's what's going to happen. By the time the second band says, "Hello, Milwaukee," you will have turned the color of a freshly boiled lobster. By the third band, you will be crawling on your hands and knees towards the medical tent. Also, the day after the show you will a) have your funniest friends slapping you on the back in mock congratulations and b) have begun a snakelike pro-

cess of molting your skin.

How do you avoid this burning sensation? It's simple. Use sun block. Use it plentifully. Put it on before the show. Reapply it during the show if you want to cover all your bets. Your skin, and everyone in the crowd who winces each time they see one of those poor red people, will thank you.

The Rastafari-Man

You would think that The Rastafari-Man, who goes through more herb than Mrs. Dash, would be a mellow concert companion, and he certainly can be. The Rastafari-Man doesn't reach a Zen-like state until he has rolled his first joint of the day. In the meantime, he's as single-minded and stressed as a businessman running late for his morning commute. First he needs to score weed. Then he has to sneak it through the doors. From there, he has to find a spot far from security and far from any potential Crowd Cops who might turn him in.

This dude has three hobbies besides working hard to get stoned: trying out cannabis-centric looks like blond dreadlocks; making like MacGyver and fashioning impromptu smoking devices (Ever used an apple as a bong? A page from a hotel-room Gideon's Bible as a rolling paper?); and experiencing ganga-inspired awe at concerts.

Don't believe me? The next time you see Metallica, you may be impressed by James Hetfield's considerable guitar chops. You can ask your Rastafari-Man friend about his experience. He isn't just sharing your admiration. Fueled by medical grade marijuana, he is having visions of old James bedecked with a halo and angel wings, while a blown-away Jimi Hendrix keeps whispering "Wow!" in his ears.

Don't go to a music festival broke

Nothing seems more rock 'n' roll than the phrase, "I'm broke, but what the hell! Who knows when I'll get a chance to see Meatloaf in concert again?" The best things in life are free, right? Think again.

If you scraped together just enough for a ticket and the only thing left in your pocket is a movie stub and a pack of Zig-Zags, you're in for a cruel wake-up. Let's say you can resist necessities like a T-shirt from the merch booth, and impulse buys like a Henna tattoo and a membership to Greenpeace. What you can't resist is the call of nature, and I'm not just talking about the beckoning of the foul-but-free porta-potty.

You've got to keep hydrated, man, and hydration costs. Forget the fact that you're too broke to hit the beer line. When the temperature rises, two things are guaranteed: a) Some dude with particularly meaty arms is going to decide to rock a tank top and b) You're going to want that frozen lemonade, you're also going to want several bottles of water, and when your body stops screaming about how thirsty you are, your stomach is going to start growling. That's when you're going to want to rip into a tofu wrap, which at that point will seem like a bargain at eight bucks.

Nine hours can seem like a lifetime; if you don't keep yourself fresh and fueled, you will enter the misery zone. People in the misery zone do weird things like start fights, ask strangers for a sip of their water, leave in the middle of the headlining act or crawl to the medical tent. Every misstep at a festival is a potential visit to the medical tent.

So if you're broke as a joke but absolutely can't miss this line-up, try to bum some cash off of someone who loves you or at least is related to you.

PRE-SHOW

Getting ready

The purse/jacket conundrum

What should you do when you're avoiding hypothermia? If you're Luke Skywalker, you slit open a dead Ton Ton and climb inside to stay warm. Most of us, however, are advised to press our bodies as close as possible to someone else. This proximity is par for the course at most concerts, so the level of body heat is measurable.

With this in mind, think twice about packing that parka. Sure, when the days turn cold that walk from your parking spot to the venue can be grueling. Just try to think ahead. You may be snug now but once you're inside, you will be faced with a warm crush of fans; that heat increases with each beer and each step closer to the surging sauna that is the mosh pit. Pretty soon the room smells like the boy's locker room in high school, a mix of damp sweat socks and Mennen Speed Stick, and you start looking for a place to stash your jacket.

There is only one time when you should consider lugging the cozy deadweight that is a jacket to a general admission show: When the gig's outside and Mother Nature is angry. Otherwise, just say no to bringing a jacket. It's better to be cold for five minutes than hot for two-and-a-half hours.

The question of whether or not to bring a purse is similar to the jacket conundrum with one exception. Many women feel naked without their purse. There's something comforting in being able to fish around among receipts, old fortune cookies, ATM statements and gum wrappers for necessities such as identification and strawberry lipgloss.

If this sounds like you, your best bet is to implement "the transfer." This is when you take concert necessities like tickets and money out of your big purse and put them in a little purse. This makes for a more streamlined concertgoer and encourages you to end the madness with a little handbag housekeeping.

The Time Cop

Among every group of friends and in every couple is a Time Cop. The Time Cop combines an avid love of music with a realistic view of concert logistics. He or she knows exactly how long it takes to get to the venue, park and find seats. The Time Cop may even throw an extra half-hour into the getting-to-the-gig timeline because we all know about Murphy's Law. If you're running late, traffic is running heavy.

The Time Cop hates being late to shows and hates waiting for other people, so this guy or gal takes as much control of the situation as possible. They buy and hold on to the tickets and usually are the ones driving to the venue. They always have cash in hand while their buddies have an endless list of errands to run, including stopping at the ATM, picking up some cigarettes at 7-Eleven and dropping off some paperwork with their tax guy at H&R Block. This drives The Time Cop crazy, because every second that The Time Cop's Whoo Crew gal pal adds another layer of hairspray and every second that his Bro-Magnon buddy spends blending pre-show margaritas, the risk of missing the opening act increases. There are few things The Time Cop hates more than getting in late when it's dark and hustling to find seats.

At first blush, it seems like Time Cops are anal retentive jerks but the truth is, they are motivated by a strong respect for the power of the live music experience, in its entirety. Plus, Time Cops make great friends because they are usually as hyper-aware of just how drunk everyone is likely to get as they are of the ticking of the clock. Because of this, they are always the designated driver. And to The Time Cop, forgoing a bit of booze is more than worth the time-control opportunities offered by being in the driver's seat.

Tailgating

The Unauthorized T-shirt Guy

The guy selling bootleg shirts at every show is kind of like a hotel concierge. He's always the first person to greet you when you arrive on the scene. He's actually a welcome sight, because concert

PRE-CONCERT
FAN MARKETING.

AFTER-CONCERT
INVENTORY ANGST.

merchandise is a bigger rip-off than an airport hot dog.

When you approach The Unauthorized T-Shirt Guy, use caution. Along with hissing at people milling around the parking lot, his most effective tactic is waving the front and back of the shirt he's hawking like a bullfighter beckoning a bull with a cape. Assuming you get his attention without being elbowed, you're liable to land a pretty good deal. You will feel righteous in getting this deal, because those $35 shirts and $60 hoodies they're selling inside represent nothing short of highway robbery.

Keep in mind, though, there is no such thing as a free lunch. Bootleg merchandise is often sub-par, so you want to take a quick gander at what you're getting. It's not just the guy's craftsmanship with his garage heat press you want to inspect. It's the quality of the T-shirt itself. Customers have been known to inadvertently buy shirts that are as broad as they are long, and these aren't good buys unless you have the physique of late-rapper Big Pun. Other tees lack staying power. Worst case scenario: Be prepared to get one good wear out of your bootleg shirt before it is filled with Pledge as you are dusting your house.

Scalping (Don't get screwed)

It's a good idea to pick up tickets from sites such as eBay or Craigslist in advance. Thanks to other people's nasty break-ups and flakey friends, you can land very good last-minute deals. What's more, outfits like eBay often offer ways to receive recourse if you get screwed.

If you don't have a ticket, you'll start to see people selling them while you're walking from your car towards the venue. You would think some of these shady characters—who look like the neighborhood watch silhouette personified—were the last people in the world you could trust. The plus with the street hawkers is that they generally have hard-copy tickets on hand. Theoretically, these could be fakes but they're a better bet than paper tickets, which can be easily duplicated... and duplicated... and duplicated.

If you do score an extra paper ticket from an accommodat-

OLD-SCHOOL
SCALPER

MODERN
SCALPER

ing stranger, try to walk into the show with him and then pay.

The Old-School Scalper (Damone)

If you've embraced the computer age, chances are you won't go to a venue without tickets. However, if you do ever show up empty-handed in the hopes of getting in, you may encounter a dying breed: The Old School Scalper. Think Mike Damone of "Fast Times," walking through the halls of Ridgemont High looking for takers on "Earth, Wind and Fire" tickets.

The Old School Scalper is a gritty sort, a take-no-prisoners guy who works and lives out of a Dodge Van emblazoned with a Houses of the Holy-inspired mural. If you asked his name, they will give you a handle that sounded distinctly unfamiliar on his tongue: "Just call me Kruiser."

Kruiser deals in wadded cash and keeps the engine running in preparation for a quick get-away, and he talks faster than a livestock auctioneer. "Let's go, let's go," he says, snapping his fingers. "I've got three guys behind you waiting for tickets." The Old-School Scalper is a master of the hard-sell because he went through hell to get tickets. This entrepreneur is willing to camp out overnight in a Buffalo blizzard if he thinks he can get his hands on front-row Stones tickets.

What's more, they have no incentive to sweet-talk customers because he has no competition. If the ticket window says "Sold Out," Kruiser is your only option. God forbid you waste his time by asking silly questions about whether your seats are located on the aisle.

The Party Posse

The Party Posse consists of the folks who make concerts a rich people-watching spectacle. They get to shows early so they can properly tailgate and, throughout the show, they catch up with friends as if they were at a high school reunion. In some ways, it is a high school reunion, because real rock partiers are loyal fans, and have been following the same bands religiously since the days

when Clearasil was part of their morning regimen.

The ultimate Party Posse members know how to whoop it up in the parking lot like no one else, whether it's passing the dutchie in the limo or making lengua tacos on a Hibachi grill.

The Margarita Whoo Crew

At every concert you will spot at least one gaggle of girls so ready to let loose you'd think they'd spent the last ten years in Kabul, wearing a head-to-toe burka with only their eyes exposed to the oppressive Taliban-ruled world. These ladies are wound up and maniacally ready to celebrate, whether the occasion be a pre-nuptial shindig, a 30-plus birthday or an appearance by a band whose greatest hits rock the entire delegation like a hurricane.

You know it's a celebration because the gals have rented a limo. With the need for a designated driver sidestepped and plenty of attention ensured, these chicks waste no time kicking the party into overtime.

First, they spend an hour in the parking lot, sticking their heads out of the window and screaming "whooooooo!" Next they walk to their seats carrying margaritas and still whooing (notice they never order beer, only margaritas).

These ladies keep half an eye on the stage, half an eye on their buds and another eye on the crowd to catch its reaction to their sexy party posse. These let's-get-drunk-and-scream ladies are an affront to music fans because they tend to nab kick-ass seats, only to talk to each other and toast the whole show. They do, however, snap to attention when they hear the bars of a greatest hit. Along with sustained whooing, dancing like there's no tomorrow—and no one else in the audience—is de rigueur. Though the tone is festive, these girls do tend to get pissed at the ushers for shooing them back to their seats time and again for dancing.

These women are hopped up on tequila until they're teetering on their high heels. What's more, they have been singing along to the Counting Crows "Mr. Jones" all the way to the show, firmly sealing their mob mentality. Shooting the requisite dirty look their way is only going to provoke a snappy retort, followed by a supportive round of "whoooos." So what is your recourse? Find your

inner filter and reach for a Zen-like focus on the stage. If this doesn't work, try to nab an unused spot in a galaxy far, far away.

The Beer Whoo Crew

If the Margarita Whoo Crew consists of girls who were cheerleaders and other in-crowd fixtures in high school, the Beer Whoo crew features the friendly girls. You know, the ones who were always welcome at parties because, by senior year, they knew how to set up a beer keg blindfolded and with one arm in a sling. They've been out of high school longer than the Margarita Whoo Crew, but they still treasure the memories, not to mention the Pink Floyd shirt they tricked out with scissors to better display their cleavage.

While Margarita Whoo Crew gets excited about a new band every year, these gals possess unwavering loyalty. They see Sammy Hagar each and every time he comes to town, and they never forget to bring enough beer money. Now in their 40s and 50s, the Beer Whoo Crew has been rocking for years so they know the

score. They pool their money months in advance to line up a limo, and it's not only because they want to enhance that special-occasion feeling. The truth is, none of these women wants to end up high and dry in the role of designated driver. Sometimes it seems as if classic rock fans, particularly members of the Beer Whoo Crew, have made a time machine, not out of a DeLorean but out of that limo they pulled up in with a collective "Whoooo!" The Beer Whoo Crew has definitely done the hair and clothing time warp. Who the hell is anyone to tell a member of the crew that she should put away the black spandex skirt she owns that is getting tighter with every concert? She wore that skirt to a Boston gig years back, and that's just the start of the good memories.

Despite a certain fashion steadfastness, the Beer Whoo Crew can offer some lessons to all of us. Have fun with your friends. Be prepared. The party ain't over 'til the sun comes up. "Whooo!" on, ladies.

The Bro-Magnon

The Bro-Magnon is an affable enough character, at least until the beer kicks in. Every concert is like a reunion of a fraternity for these guys, and we're not talking about a gathering of the Tri-Lams. The Bro-Magnon was the coolest guy in school and he hasn't lost an ounce of that radness. The main characteristic of the Bro-Magnon is that he is dying to know what's up and how it's going. You've heard the variations: "What's up, bro?"; "How's it going, man?"; "What's up, dude?"; "How's it going, dog?"

He also is dying to take his shirt off. That shirtless guy at the outdoor concert or festival? He's a Bro-Magnon.

These dudes really get stoked once they ingest a couple $10 cups of beer. They have a pair of trademark moves. One is ignoring mosh-pit boundaries. This includes dancing with a cup of beer and, in the process, sloshing barley and hops over anyone who gets too close. The other is making like a Decepticon and transforming into another concert character: The High-Five Idiot.

The High-Five Idiots

I love when you see two drunk guys sneak down and try to get better seats. The sneak-down is a rich tapestry of boldness and subtlety. High-Five Idiots mock all those who aim for seat-upgrade artistry, because they don't even try. They stumble and leap their way toward good seats like streakers at a football game. Once they find their new seats, they start high-fiving each other like crazy until the ushers move in. Their complaint is always, "Dude, there is no one else here. Let us stay." They will usually trip on your feet and spill beer on you on their way back to their nosebleed seats.

Something to think about: When should you stop calling your friends bro, man, dude and dog? Perhaps it's when you start enjoying the solo work of Rod Stewart in the 2000s as much as music by Rod Stewart in the '70s.

SHOWTIME

The Pat-Down Guy

Once, the guys who did the security check were worried about the little things—folks smuggling in weed, liquor and the paraphernalia needed to make a bootleg tape. They were usually burly longshoreman moonlighting or the occasional ass-kicking woman who resembled a road-worn American Gladiator. Their hands-on pat-down meant business. You knew that the chances were good that not only would that camera down your pants be confiscated but you would find yourself being dragged out of the venue while enduring a half-Nelson.

The consensual rape that is today's pat-down is a bit more sophisticated. With the advent of the metal-detecting wand, the teen-aged door monitor might weigh a hundred pounds soaking wet. What's more, your nether-regions may endure no more invasion than the wave of an electronic baton. All this said, security feels more serious now. This is because with video-equipped cell phones, everyone is a potential bootlegger.

What's more, the venue, and the country, have bigger fish to

fry. As unbelievable as it may sound, the Department of Homeland Security seems to have determined that the next stop for Al-Qaeda is a Barenaked Ladies show.

With this in mind, be prepared to open your purse and have a security guard of the same gender—though not necessarily the same sexual orientation—frisk you and probe you with a device that looks a lot like the ones the Ghostbusters used to detect paranormal activity. If you're going to sneak in that travel-sized bottle of Schnapps, look for booze with a non-detectible plastic cap and give a buyer-beware to your friends so they know the contraband they're enjoying has spent the last hour in your Fruit of the Looms. If you're caught, don't rage against the machine. Just smile and dump it out because no cheap buzz is worth missing a good show.

The Wonderful Wizard of Spin

One of the most mysterious of concert standbys is The Wizard of Spin. This is the guy who picks the pre-show tunes to get the party started and mans his invisible DJ booth again between sets.

No one has a clue who this guy is and yet we're at his mercy. Are we going to be forced to hear AC/DC's "You Shook Me All Night Long" for the 10 millionth time? If so, there's no one to complain to about his trite selection. If he does trot out something cool and obscure, it's not like when you're at a used record store. You can't ask, "Who is that last song by?" because there's no one to ask.

Considering that the Wiz is entertaining as many as 20,000 people, in complete anonymity, he has all the mystique of the members of KISS when no one had seen them without their make-up. In fact, he is so anonymous that he may well be wearing KISS make-up while revving up the crowd.

Meeting your idols

We all want to meet our musical heroes, or so we think. The meet and greet, which works in one of two ways, offers just such an opportunity. The pre-show meet-and-greet is a very organized setup.

Usually you have a member of the band's entourage line

you up military-style and, one by one, you get to shake the hands of musicians for about 10 seconds. It's usually a letdown because the band members are so much less enthusiastic than the fans. The band just wants to hit the stage, while the folks meeting them—who usually got this opportunity via a radio contest or because they are fan club members—have probably been practicing what they're going to say for weeks. You're usually hustled through so fast that you're lucky if you get to blurt out something reminiscent of Chris Farley's star-struck talk show host on SNL: "Remember that time you played in Indianapolis, even though it was raining? That rocked!"

A post-show meet-and-greet is a lot looser, offering more chance for interaction. The show's over, there's beer around and band members are chatting with the press, so it's much easier to approach them. This might be your chance to get into that rehearsed speech, in which you get a minute to share how that last album got you through a terrible break-up. Still, it can also be disillusioning. The worst-case scenario is that you discover your favorite singer is a pompous ass. In this case, you're going to have

> **This Magic Moment**
> "I went to a meet-and-greet back in the '90s. I shook the bands hands and was whisked out of there in five minutes but that still gave the lead singer time to look my girlfriend up and down while making fun of her Minnie Mouse voice. It is kind of weird seeing one of your idols checking out your girlfriend and knowing he could bang her if he really wanted to!"

to work mighty hard to come up with excuses for their behavior, lest you be turned off by the music that's been an integral part of your life's soundtrack. What's more likely, however, is that you'll be disappointed not by your favorite group's rock star attitude but by their very non-rock star attitude.

The older bands are usually not as active as they used to be. You step into the room expecting to encounter a rock orgy. Instead, everyone has put on their glasses and taken off their stage personas. They're reading the paper and discussing where to pick up their kids—nothing like you imagined. That is why sometimes the best policy is to go out of your way not to meet your idols. Because you don't want to go backstage only to see Tom Petty complaining about back pain and doing a Sunday crossword puzzle.

THE UPGRADE DOWNER

Upgrading seats

At some point in your concert-going career, you will find yourself holding down seats in the dim nether-regions of a venue. When you can hold up a dime and it dwarfs the lead singer's head, you can be certain you are located in the "nosebleed section."

It's true that distant seats are better than none. What's more, with the growing popularity of huge video screens at concerts, you can see each of Prince's five get-up changes or the smoke that rises from Joe Perry's fingers as he engages in some of his more furious fretwork no matter where you're seated. Things are just not the same when you're closer to the exit than to the stage. You can't "feel" the charisma that emanates from your rock heroes. Your neighbors—equally dispirited by the seats their broke asses had to settle for—seem more interested in balancing their cardboard tubs of popcorn and cups of Pabst than rocking out.

Have you ever weighed the benefits of standing up and representing at a show against the risk of pissing off your entire section, the population of which is seated as determinedly as if they were on an emergency-landing airplane with the fasten seat belts sign illuminated? That's when it's time to think about the seat upgrade.

Security is your best friend

One creative move is to take a trip to the bathroom a couple songs into the gig. Many concert attendees pound a couple of beers before a show, so it's likely you already hit the bathroom on the way in. Nevertheless, play dumb and ask the usher where the can is, making sure to look him right in the eye. Then, as you head back into your section, make sure to thank him.

At this point, the usher not only remembers your face, he sees you as a mild-mannered guy who says please and thank-you and lives by the rules. He may neglect to ask for your ticket stub as you head for an empty seat—as close to the stage as you can reasonably get. You can seal the deal by projecting an attitude like you own your shoplifted seat.

If you're motivated enough, you can take this tactic further by creeping closer and closer to the stage, like a football player inching towards a first down. Keeping a fake-it-'til-you-make-it attitude and watching out for defensive linemen like the Crowd Cop and the take-no-prisoner style usher, aim for the concert equivalent of reaching the Superbowl: sneaking all the way from the worst of the nosebleed seats to a spot so cherry that you can simultaneously reach out your arms and touch the bass player and a Concert Snob.

Giving props

You may have your sights set on a serious seat upgrade, but if you lack an air of authority, you're going to be shot down—and fast. You may want to consider some props that will help you get the wave-by. For that stylish roving security guard look, look no further than your local Wal-Mart. Nothing says, "I belong here" better than the following: a walkie-talkie, a clipboard and a flashlight.

Or, you might want to take the route a friend of mine has been abusing for years: Pretend you're a music journalist. All you need is a faux press pass including your handle, a photo and the

name of the publication with which you are affiliated. Pick something obscure yet authentic in sound, like "Rock Journal, San Francisco." It's almost failsafe.

Do use a bit of subtlety in selecting your props. Don't wear a '30s-style derby with a card saying "Press" on it. This is the equivalent of Spanky from the Little Rascals riding on Alfalfa's shoulders wearing an oversized trench coat and a fake moustache, trying to pass as a grownup. Also avoid taking a page from Carrot Top and getting too propped out. If you show up sporting a vest with a nametag and a press pass on a lanyard, plus a clipboard and a pen flashlight, you'll end up looking like a cross between a "Circus" magazine journalist and a Kinko's stock boy.

Getting "back" to the pit

When it comes to a general admission show, it's not so much a matter of proving that you have a legitimate right to sit closer to the stage. It's about pushing your way through a mass of people who are intent on keeping spots they may have staked out hours ago. Ever tried to muscle your way into a lane during L.A. rush hour? This is the musical equivalent. It's not for the faint of heart but if you've just got to get close enough to smell PJ Harvey's aggression, here are four timeworn methods.

1: Dry-heave as if you're about to become a human fountain of Guinness and Nachos Supreme. The crowd will part like the Red Sea. (Note: Nachos Supreme is more incendiary than regular nachos because, for three bucks more, your chips and orange cheese goo is enhanced with a couple pumps of Grade-D meat paste plus onions and jalapeños)
2: Start dancing clumsily with beers in each hand. The Invisible Circle effect will ensue.
3: Nod and point to your mate in the front. If you're feeling especially daring, claim that you or your girlfriend is pregnant.
4: As a last resort, start screaming or crying. People will assume you're having a very special episode of a very personal nature instead of just being a greedy fan.

THE PIT NIGHTMARE

Disorderly conduct

That Bitch (The girl fight)

Everyone knows concert horror stories, when what started as a great gig erupts in senseless violence. Think of the anarchy of Woodstock '99, or the deadly clash between Hell's Angels and flower children at Altamont in '69. Melees like these are rare. Yet, the truth is, every concert is rife with potential conflict. One of the most common clashes is the girl fight. Sorry, guys, this is not a what-if-in-the-midst-of-the-fighting-they-get-as-excited-as-we-are-and-make-out? scenario. Girl fights tend to be over two things, attitude and turf, and they're very subtle.

It's 9 p.m. and you are happily singing along with the headliner. Do you know where your girlfriend is? Look down. If she is mesmerized by the lights and the music, all is well. But, if she

looks sore as hell, it is likely she's engaged in a girl fight and, though no fists are swinging, a heated battle of the wills is underway.

Here's how it begins. A woman gets comfortably settled close to the stage, in a spot marked by the absence of The Tall Guy. Her needs are modest: a good view of the stage and an earful of music. Enter onto the scene another woman with different priorities. She has come to move—to dance, to make out with her boyfriend, to mock-mosh with her friends, to make out with her girlfriend's boyfriend, and to dance some more. Aided by beer, mind-altering substances and natural high spirits, she is insensible to those around her. Like the universe itself, she is constantly expanding. Soon, she encroaches on the magic circle that is the other woman's space.

At this point, she becomes "That Bitch." This moniker is no joke. Ask any number of peeved girlfriends what's wrong and their answer will be nearly identical: "That Bitch keeps bumping into me with her stupid backpack" or "If That Bitch elbows me one more time, I'm going to hit her."

Women rarely come to blows but it is now the prerogative of The Serious Concertgoer to ward off her exuberant neighbor at all costs. Suddenly, she is standing like a hockey goalie and wishing she were wearing shoulder pads, because That Bitch always

> ***This Magic Moment***
> "My wife is one of the mellowest people I know, but all it took was a couple behind her, chatting all through a Morrissey show, for her to lose her cool. Twenty minutes into the show, prompted by a combination of Moz worship and beer, she finally yelled, 'Shut the f--- up.' The couple moved."

becomes more aggressive when she realizes someone is trying to cramp her style. Picture a woman at a Pixies concert warding off a space-encroaching girl for two hours, armed only with a dirty look and a stiletto.

Of course, making your vast annoyance known seems paramount. It's the principle of the thing. The truth is, there is no winning this fight. After you've called That Bitch out, or after a carefully-orchestrated dance move causes you to "accidentally" elbow your nemesis back, just move to another spot. Within ten minutes, you'll forget what you were so mad about and get back into your laser-like focus on the show.

Fight Chick Girl

Most girl fights are marked by dirty looks and pointed comments—weapons of masked aggression. There is, however, one concert-going gal who doesn't mind an in-your-face altercation, The Fight Chick Girl. This is the girl who lives to get in the pit and mix it up with the guys. The Fight Chick Girl is often short (five feet seems to be the average). She tends to dress in concert camouflage such as the ubiquitous black hoodie but, much like a Chihuahua, size has little to do with her levels of aggression and boldness. That little person who just muscled you aside in a single-minded beeline to the pit? That's a Fight Chick Girl. That girl who just punched a guy because he stepped on her friend's shoe? That's a Fight Chick Girl.

Though she can be belligerent, this woman is a choice companion at shows because she'll help you get to the pit at a general admission venue every time. She uses sheer determination like a machete in the jungle, hacking her way to the front of the stage. You merely follow the trail she has blazed.

> **This Magic Moment**
>
> "I went to a Puddle of Mudd concert with a Fight Chick Girl a while back and she had a mouth like a trucker. Frustrated that the headliners only delivered a 50-minute set, she went off towards the end of the show, oblivious to the dirty looks around her. She started heckling the band, screaming things like 'F--- play your hit!' and 'If you want more fans, put out another album!' It was funny because she's so short, no one could tell where the yelling was coming from."

Picks 'n' sticks
The Guy Fight

If there's anything that can cause a melee worthy of a somber VH1 special, it's an errant drumstick or a pick flung into the crowd. Who knows whether the inevitable feeding frenzy is caused by the thrill of competition or the misapprehension that possessing a drumstick wielded by Tre Cool of Green Day will make you drum like... well, Tre Cool of Green Day.

Any time anything besides sweat flies off the stage—from picks 'n' sticks to a sweaty face towel—a hundred guys descend on the scene and struggle for ownership. Fists are flying, adrenaline is pumping: It's a highly

combustible atmosphere. It's also more than a little ridiculous. Because if you look at the dudes hustling to catch a 33-cent guitar pick, you realize that, deep down, each of them wants that triangular piece of plastic more than single women at a wedding want to catch the bouquet.

Here's the truth, guys. You're not going to be able to sell that $4 drumstick you kicked someone's ass for on eBay because you have no proof that you didn't pick it up at Guitar Center.

What's more, you're far more likely to get injured or, worse, lose your spot than to get your hot little hands on that bit of history. The next time you see a musician's implement go aerial, just let it go, man. Let it go.

Something to think about: Consider how you might use this mentality to your advantage. Perhaps you could bring a cheap pick from your local music store and toss it into the crowd as a decoy. Then, watch your path to the front of the stage open, wide and empty, before you like The Yellow Brick Road.

The Fart 'n' Dart

Sometimes the Invisible Circle is caused not by a drunken and rowdy dancer but by something far more insidious. Nothing shakes up a crowd more than the hit-and-run incident known as crop dusting.

We all have done it. It is crowded, it is warm, you have had a few beers and—uh oh!—here it comes. That fart sneaks up on you and the next thing you know you've unleashed an unfortunate combination of the kraut dog you had a half-hour earlier and whatever beer you're drinking (usually the cheaper the beer, the worse the smell, especially draft beer). We're talking the kind of gas outlawed by the Geneva Convention.

It's loud enough in the room that you don't need to worry about the sound and you don't care about the smell because you're on the move, leaving the stench—and the recriminations—behind. You just farted and darted.

This works especially well in a larger venue where you can

make an easy escape, chuckling to yourself during your two minutes of anonymous infamy. The only clue as to who perpetrated this foulest of concert fouls is the scent lingering steps behind you. In the absence of a scapegoat, most people grit their teeth and try to pretend it never happened.

Your clean getaway will only be foiled in two instances. If you have someone with you who knows your stench, you will hear them yelling behind you: "Dammit, ______, stop blowing F-bombs!" If you are in a crowded pit or general admission venue, you have committed a crime scene from which there is no escape. Shame on you! The best advice for everyone in the reeking vicinity, including you, is to breathe through your mouth for as long as possible. It's a lose-lose for everyone, especially the triggerman, because the green cloud around you is a dead giveaway.

Women commit this odiferous concert foul less often, not because they don't fart but because they desperately don't want to fart. Women pride themselves on their attractive odor so if they feel an ominous rumble, they usually go pre-emptive and dart before they fart. They'll even give up a primo spot in order to find an empty corner, where they'll look like a bashful toddler going into the corner to poop. However, if they do accidentally let loose in a crowd, they'll leave the scene faster than Carl Lewis, letting the blame fall on a sweaty Bro-Magnon. This is a clever tactic because who are you going to believe, the cute girl with lipstick and pumps or the shirtless guy balancing a box of garlic fries and a cup of Milwaukee's Best?

This Magic Moment

"I went with a friend to see Rick Springfield back in his '80s heyday. An hour into the show, Rick dedicated a song to his dad. My friend—who was now blitzed—decided to scream at people for talking over his dedication: 'He is talking about his Dad. Shut the hell up!' With his English accent, he sounded precisely like Dudley Moore in 'Arthur.' I wanted nothing more than to become invisible but that was impossible. We were wearing sleeveless white and pink RS half-shirts we'd bought before the show—not exactly inconspicuous attire."

The Loose Cannon

We all have a friend who's a bit of a

loose cannon. They're loyal as a dog and the life of the party but after a few drinks (The Loose Cannon always has a few drinks), their behavior is so unpredictable you're tempted to take a class in chaos theory just to get a handle on it.

Dr. Jekyll and Mr. Heideken (72 Ounce Warning)

The Loose Cannon can bring you a lot of unwelcome attention because most people abide by the old adage "birds of a feather flock together." Therefore, if your buddy whom you have consciously selected to be your show-going companion makes an ass of himself, you're assumed to be just as obnoxious. Your other dicey buddy, though, Dr. Jekyll and Mr. Heideken, can actually get you ejected from a show, or get you free tickets to an ass-kicking.

Dr. Jekyll and Mr. Heideken tends to change personalities after a frosty beverage or two. You see these people at shows quite a bit—the cool guy next to you who suddenly wants to kick your ass because you stepped on his shoelace. Be aware of these people,

especially in a general admission venue where you are rubbing elbows without the benefit of the safe refuge of an assigned seat.

People who bring this incendiary dude with them to a show don't want any trouble. In fact, Dr. Jekyll and Mr. Heideken doesn't want any trouble. Like most folks who can't handle their liquor, when he's in his Dr. Jekyll mode, he's one charming dude. He's got that enthused attitude about the show and he's got jokes for days so you tend to forget that the last time you went to a concert with him, you spent the entire time trying to talk sense into a sloppy drunk guy who refused to take crap from anyone, even from someone who wasn't giving him crap. When your buddy transforms into Mr. Heideken, your mantra is "Dude, it's not worth it." When your neighbor transforms into Mr. Heideken, your mantra is "Dude, this spot is not worth this crazy guy's risk-factor." In fact, the only time The Crowd Cop and overly vigilant ushers are welcome sights is when the Coors is flowing and Mr. Heideken's blood starts to boil.

The Wasted Guy

Booze and rock has always been a wedded pair. If you're going to see an act that really matters to you, you might want to consider a trial separation. That's because everyone has a story that goes like this: "Man, I was so wasted that night I don't even remember the show."

In the case of The Wasted Guy, this is the only kind of story he has to tell. He never learns from his mistakes and never plans ahead. He never knows how he's getting to a show or how he's getting back home, and he certainly never has cash. Something about

his helpless state is endearing because his buddies continue to drag him out of shows he doesn't remember.

Tobacco sins
"The Smoking Double Standard"

You know your way around the penal code: Marijuana is illegal, cigarettes are legal. Except when you are at a show, at which point the exact opposite is true. Though not as prevalent as in the free-wheeling '70s and '80s, the smoking of a joint is still considered to be a natural part of rock concert ambience. That wafting skunky-sweet smell is not enough of a nuisance to make you want to harsh the buzz of your glassy-eyed neighbors.

Cigarette smoke, on the other hand, is now cause for lynching. Maybe it's because of all the bad press on the effects of second-hand smoke. Or maybe it's because that chain-smoker looks pretentious and uptight. Whatever the reason, lighting up that Marlboro is a no-no.

In case you remain unconvinced, let me lay it out for you. Before you even light up, you'll be getting at least one serious case of stink-eye. By the third puff, the hints will have begun in earnest—coughing, pointed statements like, "Hey, man, I've got

asthma." If you don't stab out your cigarette fast, you are living on borrowed time.

If you are a dedicated smoker who wants to enjoy a gig without offending anyone, it might be wise to pick up some Nicorette gum. You might want to pick up some marijuana gum while you're at it.

The Other Lead Singer

Rock concerts tend to draw super-fans but, sometimes, there is someone so in tune with the band that he or she is literally in tune with the band. This person is The Other Lead Singer.

This is the guy or gal who throws back their head and sings along with every song; they have so much enthusiasm you're almost tempted to hand them a microphone and get it over with. If you're at a U2 show, they're all singing along to "With Or Without You." If you're seeing The Who, they are hooting like owls along with the chorus of "Who Are You?"

Whether these guerrilla karaoke performers are tone-deaf or the next American Idols, they are a truly dangerous neighbor. Because the next time one of your favorite musical gems gets stuck in your head on heavy rotation, it might just be the song as performed by The Other Lead Singer.

If you are one of these Sing-Along Sams, by all means, belt out the song in your heart. When it comes to emoting, sing a bit more softly and in tune. If your fellow fans don't want to kill you now, they'll want to kill you later. You know, that's just bad karma.

> ***This Magic Moment***
> "I'm ruined for life on certain songs because of The Other Lead Singer. For instance, I can never listen to 'Stroke Me' by Billy Squier again as long as I live. Yet, I guess, would I really want to?"

Chatty Cathies

Why on earth someone would pay seventy-five bucks to see a talented act, only to ignore the performance, is beyond most music fans? This is the MO for the Chatty Cathy. Chatty Cathy is someone whose connection with friends is so deep, and whose life is so drenched in

drama, it bears discussion at all times. She's also one of the worst concert-foul perpetrators in the book.

Here's what happens. Though occasionally Chatty Cathy shows up with a gaggle of girlfriends, she prefers to bring one special confidante to a show. No matter whom she's seeing—from the Arctic Monkeys to the Red Hot Chili Peppers—it just so happens that the gig coincides with one of her many life crises. An incident has taken place that must be aired, discussed from every angle, laughed about, cried about, and aired again. Her companion is either a fellow Chatty Cathy or a great listener; either way, she cares deeply about what her pal has to say and doesn't give a crap about what's happening on stage.

If you happen to sit in the immediate vicinity of Cathy and friend, you will be subjected to snippets of a long, egomaniacal story that lasts the duration of the concert: "So he said...and then I was all...and the next thing you know, we're like..."

Now there's no rule that says you have to be silent at a gig, as if you were studying in the library. However, when someone else's conversation spoils your good time, you get pissed fast. Most of us will grit our teeth when Chatty Cathies talk all through the opening act, contenting ourselves with a dirty look or two. (These,

CHATTY CATHIES

by the way, are highly ineffective. Chatty Cathies become unusually engrossed in their rap sessions. If you're at an Aerosmith show, Steven Tyler could leap off the stage and sit on their laps and they'd still keep talking.) Once that headliner gets on stage, mob mentality takes over.

We've all been at a gig where someone's incessant talking disgruntles an entire section. First, someone will rebuke Cathy politely, saying something like, "Hey, could you please stop talking? I'm trying to hear the show." Appreciative nods ripple through the crowd. If there *is* one characteristic common to Chatty Cathies besides verbal diarrhea, it's a capacity for outrage. She'll either ignore this comment or say something brilliant like, "It's a free country." This show of attitude is a cue to Chatty Cathy's neighbors to step things up a notch. The next time she starts in—"...and then she's like..."—someone will reach their breaking point and yell, "Shut the f--- up!" This comment meets with general approval and has even been known to elicit applause when Cathy does shut the f--- up, because she's a talker not a fighter.

She usually keeps her comments to a whisper for the rest of the show, until she receives a call on her cell phone, and then it starts all over: "Man, the people here are so rude. They're like... and I'm all..."

The You-Can-Dance-If-You-Want-To Fan

Didn't you get the memo? You're not supposed to really dance at a concert! That doesn't mean you have to stand stock-still like a guard at Buckingham Palace. Please people, contain your movements to that invisible rectangle that surrounds your body—the one with just enough space to keep you from elbowing a stranger in the face. Here's what you can do to show the love: execute a modest side-to-side sway or step-touch; bob your head in the universal "I'm digging it" gesture; stomp your feet enthusiastically; point along with the music; and clap, whistle and cheer.

Here's what you can't do: rock your head back and forth until your hair and T-shirt rain sweat on your unfortunate neighbors; dance in the aisles like you're an extra in the movie "Flashdance";

make your own mosh pit; and do just about anything that involves your hands other than cupping your beer for dear life.

This may sound a bit restrictive, particularly if the music is making you feel like doing your best imitation of a Solid Gold dancer. However, keeping in mind that things get tense in close quarters, your best bet is to keep your funk to yourself.

The Invisible Circle Guy

Fortunately, it's a rare occurrence to be singled out for a pounding from a belligerent guy in a muscle shirt or to find yourself on the receiving end of a dirty look from an uptight girl. These kinds of flare-ups can usually be avoided by following basic concert etiquette. Nevertheless, at every show, there will be a public menace

in attendance who is capable of bringing harm to anyone in his proximity, and no amount of etiquette can stop him: The Invisible Circle Guy. This is a dude who just can't handle the pyrotechnic combination of booze and enthusiasm.

At least the You-Can-Dance-If-You-Want-To Fan is attempting to perform classifiable dance moves. Although he or she is a space invader, a short walk can get you a fresh perspective, and get them out of your hair. Not so with The Invisible Circle Guy.

No matter how much room he has, he takes up more. The Invisible Circle is the area that people make around this hopelessly drunk dancer to avoid flailing arms and flying beer.

Like most concert perpetrators, The Invisible Circle Guy has no idea that anyone else exists. Oasis just kicked into high gear on "Wonderwall" and there he goes, bumping, crashing and spilling. This guy, who has a penchant for steel-toed boots, most enjoys expressing himself in the permeable border between those in the mosh pit and those avoiding the mosh pit. If you have a friend who likes to get sloppy drunk and go mobile, he is The Invisible Circle Guy.

Put Your Ass On My Shoulder

"Hey, I got a great idea sweetheart. It is a little crowded and hard to see down here on the floor. Why don't you get up on my shoulders so you can get a better view?" I love these people and you see them at every show. What are they thinking? I like to bet people around me how long it takes for security to tell these "dolts" to get down. "Excuse me sir, just want to remind you that there are ten thousand other people in the room that would also like to see the show."

The Concert Gypsy

Stevie Nicks is too enmeshed in classic rock history to be enthroned in the pantheon of Goth idols. This status is reserved for dark deities such as the gentlemen of Bauhaus, the iconic Siouxsie Sioux, obscure depressives like This Mortal Coil and mournful newcomers like Evanescence. But, the lace- and velvet-loving witchy spirit of Stevie can be found everywhere in the form of The Concert Gypsy.

Dressed in a long flowing skirt, with equally long, flowing hair, The Concert Gypsy retreats into an ethereal world of her own during live gigs. Eyes closed, she sways from side-to-side like a windblown tree, while her hands move in the kind of exotic flourishes generally confined to belly dancers. Her bizarre demeanor silently commands attention, while her layers of black mesh and velour insist she would prefer to be left alone.

Many of us have inadvertently brought The Concert Gypsy to a show (she is often quite down-to-earth in her daily life). Her companionship is unsatisfying, to say the least, because she's so "out there" you may as well have brought a woodland fairy to a gig instead of a friend. What's more, The Concert Gypsy is annoying to true sad sacks. Why? Because this tiny dancer, who is ultimately cheerful at heart, is way too happy about the fact that "Béla Lugosi's Dead."

The Make-Out Couple

You're in a packed venue, maybe even a stadium filled with thousands of people, but it doesn't matter. You only have eyes for one person, that guy or girl who you want to make babies with.

An hour ago you were squabbling over who neglected to replace the empty toilet paper roll in the bathroom, but once the music starts, something magic happens. Your relationship suddenly takes on a level of heat only seen in prom-night parking lots and rock videos starring Tawny Kitaen.

If you haven't been too busy sucking face yourself, you've seen this couple, locked lip-to-lip, tongue-to-tongue, oblivious to all but their epic make-out session. Sometimes the attention of these lovers seems to snap back to the stage; the lady is leaning dreamily against her man, singing along with The Killers' "Mr. Brightside." Even if you take a closer look at this seemingly innocuous pose, you'll see that the passion has only intensified. This love machine doesn't just have his arms wrapped around his girlfriend. His groin is pressed firmly into her backside, and it's stiffer

than a drumstick. It's couples like this that inspired the first heckler to shout, "Get a room!"

The younger the make-out couple, the more leeway their seatmates and neighbors give them. We all know the teen- and college-aged set are slaves to their coursing hormones, but—at the risk of sounding ageist—the older the couple, the more disturbing the bump and grind.

So, if you look more like Neil Young than Justin Timberlake, just say no to bringing sexy back. If you look more like Ann

Wilson circa 2007 than Ann Wilson circa 1977, just say no to going crazy on your friend. In other words, "Get a room!"

Something to think about: If you see the make-out couple six months later, will they still be playing tongue-hockey? Will they even be holding hands?

The Crowd Cop (Cindy Brady syndrome)
Remember cute little Cindy? She was the Brady kid who, once you got past the adorable lisp and pigtails, had a pathological need to tattle on her siblings when they were up to no good. Unfortunately, there is a Cindy Brady at every show, the guy/girl who considers it their mission to keep every gig show as wholesome as "The Brady Bunch."

The Crowd Cop used to be the kid who would tell the teacher what happened when the teacher had to step out for a minute: "Mr. Jones, Jimmy threw spit wads at me when you left the room."

This guy or girl is just as vigilant about reporting wrongdoings, but now it is the usher who is their ally.

You have a joint. Cindy turns you in! You have Bacardi in a plastic bag down your pants to save some cash and want to pour it into your 44-ounce Coke. Cindy turns you in! (By the way, nobody goes to a show and buys a 44-ounce Coke unless they have liquor to add to it.)

Cindy is usually a guy, because women do not want their asses kicked for narcing, unless they're a "fight chick girl." This righteous dude pays full price and comes to the show with his shirt tucked in and proceeds to his seat in an orderly fashion. He doesn't watch the show much because he's so busy policing the crowd. The scary thing is, Cindy could actually get you a few nights in jail rather than just a visit to the principal's office. If you want to upgrade your crappy seats and get away from this menace to benignly law-bending society, don't even think of sneaking down around Cindy. If The Crowd Cop spots you, you're toast!

The Play-That-One-Song Guy

The next time you go to a Nine Inch Nails concert, it might happen that Trent Reznor tries to catch you before the show: "Pssssst! I'm having a hell of a time coming up with a set list. Any ideas?" It might also happen that you find a golden ticket the next time you tear into a Wonka bar.

It's time for a reality check. The group you're seeing has been playing together long before you became their greatest fan. By the time a touring band hits Your Town, USA, they have perfected a mixture of new material, oldies but goodies and radio hits. The musicians do not need or want you to yell out requests. The audience does not need or want you to yell out requests.

What's more, the decision to be The Play-That-One-Song Guy is rife with potential concert fouls. Whether it's the beer talking or innate oblivion, this self-appointed MC has been known to request a song that's already been played. He also has a tendency to confuse the song's chorus with its title: "Hey, play that f--- you like an animal song!"

If you are The Play-That-One-Song Guy, and this rule seems rather harsh, you can take consolation in the fact that you do have the power to hear whatever song you want on demand. After the show, go home. Set up shop next to your CD player and get out your stack of albums by the band you just saw. Then, enjoy yelling out requests to your heart's content: "Hey, play that head like a hole song!" Then pop in "Pretty Hate Machine" and savor your my-wish-is-your-command power.

The Nokia Cinematographer

Wow! You're telling me your phone takes pictures? It even records snippets of video? So that's why you're giving yourself tennis elbow from holding your Motorola aloft, dodging rock-blockers who stumble into the crosshairs of your two-inch frame. I ask you, though: Did you really spend $75 bucks to toil as some band's unpaid videographer?

There are a couple of problems with being a post-modern

Ansel Adams. First, it's hard to enjoy a gig when you're on the job. Second, though you might get some nice close-ups of you and your pals looking like shiny, happy people, it's guaranteed that your band pics and that three-minute rockumentary you're filming are going to look like crap.

You can see from the giant video screens that Berlin's Terri Nunn is still smoking hot. However, in those photos you manage to grab from your cell, she will look like a smoking hot ant before which a sea of ants is enthusiastically hopping. The show may sound great, but when you play back that vid you took, you're going to get sick from your own shaky Blair Witch-style hand-cam. Instead of hearing Terri's lovely voice, you're going to be besieged with crowd ambience ranging from "whooo!" to somebody sneezing to that weird dude next to you singing "Sex (I'm a...)" in a baritone. Don't even think of uploading this disgrace to cinematography onto YouTube unless you're ready for some seriously snarky comments.

Dude, true memorabilia hounds and pirates smuggle in Nikons with zoom lenses and high-end digital video cameras. The really cool people with an audio/visual calling will find jobs where they are asked and paid to capture history.

So by all means, snap a few pics of you and your buddies. Hold your phone up high and indulge yourself with one Hail Mary-style stage shot. Feel free to catch a surreptitious photo of your super-hot neighboring fan, but for God's sake, after that, shove the phone in your pocket. After all, lots of opportunities open up when you punch yourself off the phone-zone time clock. You could: actually watch the concert in real-time; actually have fun with your friends instead of taking myriad pictures that make it look like you were having the time of your life; and maybe even have a word with that good-looking neighbor.

Rock and Dial

Rage Against the Machine has reunited and is whipping the crowd into a frenzy. This song is not just for the "People of the Sun"—it's for everyone who has ever raged against the status quo. Everyone knows pleasure is better when shared, so what do you do? You call up your best buddy or your significant other to give them a treat, a taste of rock history they can enjoy from the comfort of their couch.

There are a couple of problems with this scenario. First, you just might piss off your pal. He or she probably would be at the show if their checking account hadn't been overdrawn. So in this case, getting the famous "Yo, check this shit out!" call is high-tech equivalent of a schoolyard taunt: "Na, na, na, na, na—I'm here and you're not."

What's more, the set that's rocking your socks off sounds like the seventh level of hell on the phone. Your friend hears you shouting excitedly; then your voice ceases as you hold up your cell like a beacon. That's when the chaos really begins: a hint of music and a roaring onslaught of crowd sounds. This is followed by 10 more seconds of you shrieking, then more ear-punishing ambience. There should be T-shirts with slogans like, "My friend went to see Social Distortion and all I got was a lousy cell phone call." If you really want to share the magic, pony up a few bucks and buy your phone buddy some concert merch. They'll thank you for it.

LOGISTICS

Catch you later

Here's some great advice for those of you who say to pals, "Hey, I'll meet you at the show." Don't ever say, "Hey, I'll meet you at the show." Because unless you are at an arena gig and have adjoining seats—or you're heading to a small bar or club—you are not going to find your friends. No matter how distinctive your pals are (brightly dyed hair, piercings, tattoos), it is guaranteed that a large venue will be crammed with similarly distinctive people; it doesn't help that everyone is wearing black.

Cell phones are not much help. Assuming your companion's cell phone reception holds out, you'll find yourself shouting over a cacophonous combination of crowd sounds and music:

"Hey, where are you at? I'm near the front of the pit, near the speakers."

"I'm at the misting tent, cooling off. I'll see you in a minute."

Your fellow phone-tagger's minute will turn to 15 as they force themselves, like a salmon swimming upstream, to speakers at the front of the stage. But, guess what? There's been some miscommunication (there always is when you try to catch someone later) and they're at the opposite side of the pit. Then, the phone calls and the waving starts all over. You don't go to a gig to work this hard!

If you want to party with a friend at a show, drive with them—heck, make them be the designated driver. If you *do* show up to a concert with someone, hang on for dear life. Because you don't want to end up on your cell phone saying, "I'm waiting in line at the porta-potties. Where are you?"

Beer and Bathrooms

The Concession Stand Tap-Master

I wonder if the Concession Stand Tap-Master feels guilty when they ask for twelve bucks a beer with a straight face. I think they do, because their silent request for tips always seem so half-assed.

They take a plastic jar—or worse, just prop up one of the beer cups—and write the word "tips" on it with a Sharpie. Then they toss a wadded-up dollar bill in there, hoping it will serve as a talisman to draw more money.

No one ever really prepares for the price of beer and merchandise at a gig. The high prices at concerts are like childbirth: Once it's over, we tend to forget the pain and only remember the moments of joy. As a result, those who like a little Budweiser with their concert rarely tip.

We rationalize this oversight because the beer is so expensive—"I won't spend another dollar on my beer runs until the price is lowered." The real reason is we stiff the concession stand guy because we ran out of money, plain and simple. Just ask your buddy who just fished some change out of his pocket so you could afford more alcohol.

As a result of his tip-less state, and his knowledge that each beer costs more than he makes an hour, the concession stand guy often is a bit surly. If you do get fast service with a smile, there is only one explanation: He is dipping into the brew himself. He rationalizes this move because the beer is so expensive.

Breaking the seal

This is known to many as the first urination of the evening. Popular belief holds that once you "break the seal" or pee for the first time, you will repeatedly have to go throughout the show. While there are health implications of "holding it," if you can time your beer-to-bathroom ratio, trips will be fewer and you will not have to miss much of the concert.

Beer-to-bathroom ratio

If you plan to drink at the tailgate or drink in the venue, then it's time to take heed of the art form of the beer-to-bathroom break ratio. Knowing the bladder tugging facts may inspire you to chug a bit less and thus minimize the time you spend in the restroom at your chosen concert. There is a standard time frame in which one can estimate how many trips to the restroom you will have to make, according to how many alcoholic beverages you drink, to wit:

- One beer per hour =
1-2 bathroom breaks within 50 minutes

- Two beers per hour =
2-4 bathroom breaks within 50 minutes

- Three beers per hour =
3-6 bathroom breaks within 40 minutes

- Four beers per hour =
4-12 bathroom breaks during the whole show

Slap me some skin: Every man's nightmare

Men, using the bathroom while catching a popular act is a sticky wicket, literally. Inevitably you're going to meet up with that ex co-worker, high school classmate or erstwhile drinking buddy and he's going to be pumped to see you, and why not? The show is great, the beer's flowing and, dude, he hasn't seen you since that show at The Forum.

Like any good mate, he proffers his hand for you to high-five, shake or both. The problem is, the last thing he has shaken is his bare member in his now unwashed hand. What's a guy who's friendly but uncomfortable with this two degrees of separation to do? Shove your hands in your pockets and dis your buddy? Explain that you have germ-phobia and sound like you're getting a little weird in your old age?

You're not the first person to sweat this situation. Why do you think the Japanese bow when greeting each other? They've known for years about the man-I-really-want-to-show-some-love-for-my-homie-but-he-just-got-done-using-the-head conundrum. Try bowing respectfully the next time you see one of your friends.

He'll be so caught up in beer-hazed, music-crazed enthusiasm that it's likely he'll bow back, no questions asked. He'll bow the next time he sees a friend and the next thing you know, this whole bros bowing at each other thing will go viral. East meets west, man. East meets west.

The When-You-Gotta-Go-You-Gotta-Go Girl

Women, there are times when being a woman just isn't fair. This includes when you are suffering the pain of cramps or childbirth, fanning yourself with the program because you're getting hot flashes, and when you're waiting for the bathroom.

We've all seen it. The men's room is a brisk locale that, like an assembly line, spews out a continuous stream of satisfied-looking customers, zipping up and moving on. The women's bathroom, on the other hand, looks like a Depression-era breadline—long, slow moving and filled with grim faces.

Until your local stadium catches on to the age-old truth that

. . . .CLEAR

women take longer and ups the bathroom ratio accordingly, there's not much you can do.

However, you might want to hit the bathrooms a bit early to avoid the flush-rush. That's partially what opening bands are for. That's also why nearly every band has one song that doesn't make you flick your Bic—why bands like to noodle with new material when you've basically come for a live best-of.

Desperation calls for desperate measures. When a woman has had a few $12 cups of beer and the line to the ladies room stretches for miles, she has been known to appeal to a guy to help sneak her into the men's room. This move calls for a cooperative effort, because this interloper needs a sympathetic guy to stand sentinel while she pees. If you don't have a male escort handy, this is the one time when wearing those heels—the ones you'll be carrying on the walk back to your car—pays off. Because for some reason, men are more likely to come to the aid of a woman in distress when she's dressed like Kelly Bundy.

AFTERSHOW

It ain't over 'til it's over

The aftershow is an entire experience in itself, but c'mon, don't launch into it while the gig's still going!

Ben Franklin famously defined insanity as "doing the same thing over and over and expecting different results." Obviously, this clever founding father had been to myriad rock shows and observed the most insane of concertgoers, the fan who can't get it through his or her head that the concert is not over until the houselights go on and the fat lady stops singing.

Dig if you will a picture: You're at a huge venue, finally getting the chance to see The Police in action. The concert is ostensibly over, with the band having taken a much-deserved bow. Still, you're left with that not-quite-sated feeling, as if you had a light supper when you were really looking to stuff your face. What's more, you have yet to sing along with "King of Pain" and "Wrapped Around Your Finger." What do you do?

If you are as clever as good old Ben, and if you have learned from every show you've gone to, you stand up and make some noise. It's time to stomp your feet, clap your hands until they're sore and cheer yourself hoarse. You know the score: You let a band know you want more and they give you more.

Then there are those whose first priority seems to be a half-hour of extra time and an at-all-costs avoidance of human gridlock. At the end of the show, these folks scurry toward the exits—significant other in tow—like ants on the run from a can of Raid. *Wait!* Suddenly, just as they hit the stairs, the crowd goes wild. By the time Sting notes that there is a black spot on the sun, these fast-track fans are now either scrambling back to their seats or hearing a can't-miss performance from a decidedly awkward vantage. They've made a mistake, and it's one you were mentally noting as soon as the band said its first goodnight.

To those of you with a practical bent, don't give into the temptation to beat the traffic. You've waited to see this band, got a second mortgage on your home to land tickets, hauled your ass all the way to the city center and paid $20 bucks to park your car in a near-ghetto.

Make one more sacrifice and join the cheering section. Because it's virtually guaranteed that the show ain't over 'til it's over.

The Seven-Minute Rule

There is only one legitimate reason to leave your seat before the encore and that is the call of a groaning bladder. If you time it correctly, however, following the Seven-Minute Rule, you won't miss much.

There is a golden moment, if you will, that is perfect for taking that long-awaited leak—a window of opportunity in which you can miss the long lines without missing the act. The next time you go to a show, particularly a large arena gig, glance at your watch when the band finishes its "last song." A few anal-retentive folks will begin hotfooting it to their cars, looking to beat traffic, but most people will start showing the love and making the noise.

There's a bit of tension in the air. Will the band be back out for the encore everyone's demanding? Of course they will, because the houselights have yet to come on. Still, a cat and mouse game ensues in which the crowd becomes one large pep-rally, stamping their feet and screaming for the band to come out. We all think that the band decides to come back because we are so enthused. Really, they only left the stage in the first place to heighten the drama. They're not checking an applause-meter to determine when to come back. They're changing their sweaty shirts, gulping down water and beer, and maybe even sucking on an asthma pump.

Whatever the case, the band's brief hiatus always takes seven minutes.

This provides just enough time for savvy fans to jog to the bathroom—which is relatively empty at this point—and relieve their groaning bladders, then jog back to their seats in time for the encore. After the band plays that last three songs or so, and everyone files out, you'll see the fruits of poor planning in the form of folks lining up at the bathroom in droves, as if free cash were coming out of the toilet paper dispensers. You, in the meantime, are free to go out into the crisp night air unencumbered. P is for planning!

The I-Told-You-So Couple

Ladies, we know that a rock concert is a time you want to look your hottest. You might want to think twice about the kind of heels that inspired bearded rockers ZZ Top to sing "She's Got Legs." Keep in mind that you may have to walk quite a ways from your parking spot to the venue. Once a great show gets started, it's likely that no one will be sitting down. Add some exuberant dance moves, the requisite encore stomp and a walk back to your car and you're likely to feel like you're walking on raw meat at the end of the night. The next thing you know, you're limping barefoot on the sidewalk, carrying those sizzling shoes. If that's not bad enough, you'll also have to hear your guy giving you grief the whole time because he told you so.

You might want to opt for more comfortable flats, with

some arch support, or some stylish boots. However, if you can't pass up the chance to channel Barbie, don't worry. There will be plenty of women limping their way to their cars right along with you. Think of your sore, blistered feet as a badge of courage.

Land of the Lost (Dude, where's my car)

Here's the problem with concert parking. You're usually running late, plus you're amped about the show. As you dash toward the venue, you take a moment to do some cursory triangulation: "I'm in section 13, parked next to a white Grand Marquis."

It's not until the end of the concert, when you're sleepy and footsore (especially if you insisted on wearing those heels), that you realize that there is a section A13, and a section B13, and a C13, and a D13.

At first, you and your buddies share a laugh about your concert mishap, but after wandering a dozen parking areas that are basically parallel universes, you begin to suspect that you will never find your car. The Grand Marquis is long gone and you start to get that desperate, shipwrecked look.

This Magic Moment

"I lost my car at the annual Coachella music festival and have never been so happy to see a security dude riding around in a golf cart. But he was only one man, trying to help a hundred desperately lost people, all of whom parked somewhere next to a 4-Runner. In the end, all he could offer me was a sip from his canteen and an amulet bearing the likeness of St. Christopher, the patron saint of travel. I found my car an hour later."

The only landmark that looks vaguely familiar is that same Unauthorized T-Shirt Guy you saw selling smudgy Bad Religion shirts hours ago. Now he's desperate and only packing XXL merchandise, which he's willing to part with for five bucks. You consider buying a tent-sized shirt but now you're too exhausted to do anything besides keep up your death march.

You may ask, why don't concert venues take a cue from Disneyland, and make their parking sections conspicuous? Wouldn't it be nice to say with authority, "I'm parked in Mickey 14A." First of all, they'd run into some trademark issues. Second of all, you'd be so late and amped, you'd still only remember that you were parked somewhere in Mickey next to a Grand Marquis.

With this in mind, consider taking 30 seconds to get your bearings before hitting a show. Because you don't want to end up in the Land of the Lost.

Car: "Man, again my owners can't find me after a show! This is the second festival this week."

Porta-potty: "Please, you think YOU have problems? I haven't been cleaned out since Woodstock II!"

CURTAIN CALL

TWO YEARS LATER...

The You-Can-Dance-if-You-Want-To Fan
The You-Can-Dance-If-You-Want-To Fan slipped in her own beer and became a quadriplegic. Rather than viewing the accident as a tragedy, she became the producer of a television series called "Wheelchair Dancing With the Stars," which airs on public access in Raleigh, North Carolina. Contestants have complained that her moves are too extreme for the small sound set in which it is recorded.

The Wonderful Wizard of Spin
The Wonderful Wizard of Spin continues to hide behind the mask, so to speak. If you look hard enough behind the curtain, he may be found sporting Vinnie Vincent face paint, complete with an Egyptian ankh drawn on the T-section of his face. (Vincent was the first guitarist to replace Ace Frehley back in the '80s). He recently warmed up the crowd for Evanescence, starting the party off with "Hotel California."

The Whoo Crews
After a frightening tailgating incident in which both whoo crews nearly ran out of alcohol, the ladies joined forces, parking their limos side-by-side. They mixed the dregs of their beer and margaritas together, creating a drink called a Mar-beer-ita. They later got a patent on the combo, and became millionaires. They blew it all on booze and limousines.

The When-You-Gotta-Go-You-Gotta-Go Girl
After sneaking into the men's room at a Bon Jovi concert, The

When-You-Gotta-Go-You-Gotta-Go Girl sued the city of Detroit. A jury agreed that she picked up a strange rash from the men's toilet seat. She is now the spokeswoman for an organization called TASK (Tackling Atypical Skin Conditions).

The Wasted Guy

The Wasted Guy is working on a book about his rock concert experiences, from Altamont to Lollapalooza. Its working title is "How Did I Get Here?"

The Time Warp Guy

After getting a new girlfriend, The Time Warp Guy turned off his classic radio station and went on to expand his music repertoire. Unfortunately, his new gal is twenty years older than him. He divides his time between listening to The Doors "Soft Parade" and "Mel Tormé Swings Shubert Alley."

The Time Cop

The Time Cop experienced a peak moment when she won a "Brunch with Paul McCartney" radio competition. She stayed up late poring over the Thomas Guide, and picking out the perfect outfit in which to enjoy lobster and champagne with Paul. In all the excitement, she forgot the next day was "spring forward" daylight savings time. The Time Cop arrived an hour late to the event rendezvous, just in time to see the winners' bus pull away. She now practices transcendental meditation, claiming it helps her stop fixating on time.

The Tall Guy

The Tall Guy is the vocalist for a rap-metal band called Abrasion, which has headlined several Sausagefests. He doesn't have to take any more crap for blocking the view of fans but, because of his prodigious height, no one has ever seen the band's drummer and bassist.

The Supportive Girlfriend
After reading "He's Just Not That Into You," the supportive girlfriend discovered women. She swore she would never see a concert again for a guy's sake and organized a woman's music festival. Last week she was spotted at a Melissa Etheridge concert, maneuvering a Sharper Image shiatsu wand over her oblivious girlfriend's back.

The Sausagefest/Gal Pals
After someone screwed up, The Sausagefest and The Gal Pals were booked for the same weekend at the same fairgrounds. Hard metal bands and singer-songwriters took the stage over the course of the event—it sounded a lot like the first Lollapalooza. Research done since has concluded that 322 babies were conceived during the two-day concert.

The Rock Lobster
The Rock Lobster attended his 10-year high school reunion the day after a blazing summer music festival. A former halfback, he was heartily slapped on the back by a dozen Eisenhower High School football team alumni. He is now fanatical about applying sun block.

Rastafari-Man
The Rastafari-Man was busted for cultivating cannabis in the bathroom of his one-room apartment. He claimed the incident was a message from Jah, telling him to stop smoking weed. He now works at the headquarters of Isotoner Corp., where he has become a master of the Excel spreadsheet. He is physically unable to start his day until he has scored a Starbucks Carmel Macchiato with two extra shots of espresso, smuggled it into the building and found a private spot in which to enjoy it.

The Play-That-One-Song Guy
Finally got out of intensive care after getting beat up by a super-fan at a Doobie Brothers gig. His assailant he explained to a jury: "He kept screaming 'Play "What a Fool Believes," Michael!' over and over. Michael McDonald hasn't played with the Doobies in over a decade, and they've basically retired that song." He was acquitted.

The Porta-Potty
After taking a pounding at Lollapalooza, the porta-potty put in a request for a transfer to the Philharmonic, only to discover that wine and brie are as combustible a combination as beer and nachos.

The Pat-Down Guy
The pat-down guy worked a Harry Potter Convention the day after a Nickelback concert. Confused, he frisked a young attendee too vigorously. His "You never know what could be hidden beneath those robes" defense did not work. He is currently serving prison time while working towards his GED.

The Unauthorized T-Shirt Guy
After a tip from The Crowd Cop, The Unauthorized T-Shirt Guy was busted at a Barry Williams mall gig. After a successful day of selling $5 "Brody Brunch" T-shirts, he was pulled over by the mall police for tooling through a parking lot at seven miles per hour; the speed limit was five. Armed only with walkie-talkies, the rent-a-cops confiscated his heat press and 200 blank T-shirts manufactured in Jakarta.

The Other Lead Singer
The Other Lead Singer has a gig hosting karaoke every Tuesday night at Sheila Stein's Senior Life Retirement Community in Sarasota, Florida where she is known for singing at the same time as the residents. She encourages everyone to participate but has yet to turn on anyone's microphone except her own.

The Old-School Scalper
The Old-School Scalper got his van and laptop stolen by some groupies at a Hannah Montana show.

The Nokia Cinematographer/ The Rock Dialer
The Nokia Cinematographer and The Rock Dialer met at a Kings of Leon concert and, after a whirlwind courtship, got married in Vegas. The bride annoyed everyone in the

chapel, including the minister, by insisting on calling her friends on her cell phone: "Oh my God, you'll never guess what I'm doing." This sentimental duo enjoy watching their wedding video, which consists of shaky footage that can only be viewed on a three-inch screen.

The Make-Out Couple

The Make-Out Couple broke up during the encore because, after making out for three straight hours, he refused to share a straw when drinking from the same soda cup.

The Loose Cannon

The Loose Cannon went on to operate two flourishing companies in Altensteig, Germany. Located side-by-side, one is a mega phone company, the other a brewery. By 3 o'clock, he is usually drunk and slurring a loud harangue into a megaphone. Locals have begun calling that time of day Errgrimpt Zeit or "The Angry Hour."

The I-Told-You-So Couple

After repeatedly begging his wife not to wear heels to any more concerts, the guy—tired of hearing his wife complain about blisters—decided to get even. He wore ripped jeans, flip-flops, and a T-shirt to her sister's wedding.

The Invisible Circle Guy

The rowdy guy responsible for The Invisible Circle at some 300 concerts hit rock bottom, literally, while attempting to crowd-surf at a Harrah's Lake Tahoe Starship concert. When he got out of the hospital, he realized rock concerts were "totally toxic" for him. Now a New Age music aficianado, he recently got kicked out of a Yanni concert when—after drinking too much Riesling—he attempted to start his own mosh pit.

Indie Guru

The Indie Guru ran into a depressing streak when all of her favorite obscure bands, one after the other, gained worldwide notoriety. After collapsing in a state of nervous exhaustion, during which she could only croak "they sold out," she picked up the pieces and formed her own band. They were discovered by A&R reps from Sony the next day.

The Fight Chick Girl/The Concert Gypsy

The Fight Chick Girl and the Concert Gypsy experienced "soul convergence" at a spiritual retreat in Sedona, Arizona. They started a mall chain called "Blazing Issue" catering to gothic ethereals and rock bratz. Their most popular item is the Druid Hoodie, a hooded cape emblazoned with the store's logo, a fairy in combat boots. On the day of the store's IPO, their stock rose higher than that of rock-outfitters Hot Topic.

The Fart 'n' Darter

The Fart 'n' Darter went on to win a chili cook-off in Hatch, New Mexico, the chili capital of the world. Four hours of chili and beer later, he slipped into a Big Bad Voodoo Daddy show.

The Embarrassed Daughter

The Embarrassed Daughter now helps run her parents' "Seniors Rock!" clothing line. Wilford Brimley is the head spokesman.

Dr. Jekyll and Mr. Heideken

Dr. Jekyll and Mr. Heideken quit drinking after he picked a fight with The Security Guy, who drop-kicked him across the entire width of the mosh pit. When he still continued to change moods at a dizzying pace, he was diagnosed as bi-polar. He is now an indie director whose work has been called "both detrimental and dazzling" by "Rolling Stone" magazine's Peter Travers.

The Divorced Guy/
The Creepy Old Guy

The Divorced Guy and The Creepy Old Guy were placed in contiguous seats at a performance by the Neil Diamond tribute band Super Diamond. They came out of the closet soon after and are now lovingly restoring their Craftsman-style house.

The Desperately Hip Crowd

Members of The Desperately Hip Crowd lost their luggage on a flight to Germany where they planned to see The Strokes perform. Financially unprepared to replace their skinny jeans and ironic "Chicago" T-shirts, they were forced to settle on sweatpants and tourist tees bearing slogans like "Ich Lieb Deutschland!" They were so traumatized by the fashion cold winter that they are now even more desperately hip. They are currently rocking the latest trend: men's legwarmers.

The Crowd Cop

The Crowd Cop got busted for bringing his own five peeled shrimp in a baggie into a local Phoenix, Arizona La China restaurant. His defense was that "only five shrimp in a dinner portion of Kung Pao is ludicrous." His customer-of-the-year

picture was removed from the lobby and he is doing his community service as a volunteer policeman at a Beverly Hills nursing home.

The Concession Stand Tap-Master

Disgusted by the ridiculous cost of beer at concerts, The Concession Stand Tap-Master quit his job and got a new position at a large coffeehouse chain. It makes him nervous that a cup of coffee costs more than a gallon of gas but then again—since he's been dipping into the highly-caffeinated brew—everything makes him nervous.

The Chatty Cathies

The Chatty Cathies joined the cast of the "The View."

The Car in the Land of the Lost

The Car in the Land of the Lost was never found, nor was the Grand Marquis next to which it was parked.

The Bro-Magnon

Inspired by the movie "City Slickers," The Bro-Magnon went on to found a dude ranch. He can be found roaming the premises shirtless, castrating cattle and finding out "what's up" with all his guests.

Broke Festival Guy

The Broke Festival Guy got frustrated because of always being broke, robbed a Chick-fil-A in Denison, Iowa and is now serving four years in a minimum security prison. He loves it because he gets three meals a day and, most importantly, is kept hydrated.

The Air Guitar Guy

The Air Guitar Guy gained fame beyond his wildest dreams after a propitious Van Halen concert. Eddie Van Halen sprained a finger during a complicated lick and The Air Guitar Guy jumped on stage and grabbed his axe. Having seen the band in concert 200 times—playing vicious air guitar along with every song from "Ain't Talkin' 'Bout Love" to "Right Now"—he proved the perfect understudy. He is currently being groomed as a replacement for Eddie, who hopes to eventually hang up his guitar strap and retire to the Hamptons.

PEACE
NO AIR GUI

AR
ALLOWED
A.W.'07